With My Best Wishes
and May wished you
enjoy "Hit your 2nd shot
1 st." Your Friend
Marshall Smith

HIT YOUR SECOND SHOT
FIRST

FIRST EDITION PUBLISHED IN 1999 BY
THE K.I.S.S. GROUP
Commerce, OK. 74339

Library of Congress Cataloging in Publication Data
PRINTED IN THE USA
BY SUN GRAPHICS INC.

FIRST EDITION
10-9-8-7-6-5-4-3-2-1
ISBN 0-9671291-0-9

All worldwide rights reserved by
THE KISS GROUP PUBLISHING CO.

HIT YOUR SECOND SHOT
FIRST

AND OTHER SECRETS OF THE KISS METHOD
by Marshall Smith
Golf's best Kept-Secret
with Tom Ferrell

DEDICATION

"For all the wonderful people, beautiful places and fantastic stories one gets to share. Thank you Golf."

ACKNOWLEDGEMENTS

I would like to acknowledge the following people who have been instrumental in both life and the game of golf.

I would like to thank my wife Corinne and my children Corinne, Christy, Cathy, Elizabeth and Marshall Jr.

It is impossible to name all the friends I have made along the way, but I must name some. Ky Lafoon my mentor. Mickey Mantle, my best friend, and the wonderful people I met with him through the years.

Chi Chi Rodriguez, Walt Zembriski, Craig Stadler and so many other pros including an up and comer named Matt Gogel. Thanks to Walt Newls, Otis Winter, Dick Dela Cruz, Steve Owens, Bill Grigsby, Dale McNamara, and so many pupils and friends who have made my life so blessed.

Finally, Tom Ferrell for putting my thoughts and ideas on paper., Elizabeth Girard for editing; the world famous artist Nick Leaskou for the magnificent drawings and the outstanding cover; and Eugene Rexwinkle for all his help in getting this book printed.

FOREWORD

Marshall Smith has been a teaching pro for more than 50 years. During those years he has worked with some of golf's top touring professionals. Gary Player, Craig Stadler, Chi Chi Rodriguez and Walt Zembriski are just a few who have come to Marshall for advice. However, Marshall's favorite students are the junior golfers. He's worked with youngsters through clinics, schools and charity tournaments. His simple eloquence has brought the love, etiquette and rules of the game to hundreds who will never forget his advice. Marshall has met and played with many of the greats. Ky Lafoon was a legendary golfer of the 1930's and 40's and Marshall's mentor. Many of the lessons he learned were from Ky. He still loves to regale listeners with stories of these personalities.

Mickey Mantle, Marshall's best friend from his early Oklahoma days was also his student. It was only through golf that Mickey found the enjoyment and serenity that was so elusive throughout his life.

As you read Hit your Second Shot First heed the instructions, but also enjoy the stories of golf pros and amateurs scattered throughout. We hope you learn to appreciate the beauty of a course as only Marshall can describe and that through his lessons you will find your best game.

The Publishers

TABLE OF CONTENTS

Foreword

Chapter 1   Hit Your Second Shot First

Chapter 2   The Lesson Tee

Chapter 3   Long Game Lesson

Chapter 4   Practice That Works

Chapter 5   The Golf Course

Chapter 6   Course Management

Chapter 7   Driving The Ball

Chapter 8   Get Out of Jail

Chapter 9   Etiquette: The Golfers Code of Respect

Chapter 10 The Rules of Golf

Chapter 11 Competition

Chapter 12 The 19th Hole, Reflections On The Game

CHAPTER 1

Hit Your Second Shot First

The problem with golf instruction is that it makes a simple game hard. How many times have you duffed a shot, dropped a second ball, and then hit a shot the tour pros would have been proud of? The reason is because you didn't put any pressure on yourself the second time around – you kept it simple. You stopped thinking about how to swing and you simply swung. "Hit your second shot first" is the best piece of advice I've ever received. That's why I'm giving it to you now.

I've been teaching golf for more than 50 years. I've taught beginners, junior players and players on the PGA, LPGA, and Senior tours. My philosophy toward golf is the same one that has built many a successful business: Keep It Simple Stupid (KISS). Most of the time, the answer to a problem is just as easy to spot as a pair of ruby red lips. It's the same with golf.

I've seen all the fads come and go. I've seen flat swings. I've seen upright swings. I've seen short swings, long swings, fast swings and slow swings. But if you boil it all down, there's only one thing that all good players have in common, and that's balance. If you're looking for a secret, there it is. If you can combine power and balance, you can hit the ball long and straight. Sounds easy enough, right? It is, but it takes discipline and commitment to train your body to make a simple, balanced move during the golf swing. You have to master the fundamentals we'll discuss in this book, and once you do you'll be on your way to enjoying a game that will last a lifetime, open up doors, and make you a member of every generation that comes before and after you. In other words, you'll come to love golf the way I do.

Feel Your Way

When I learned the game, instruction was different from what it is

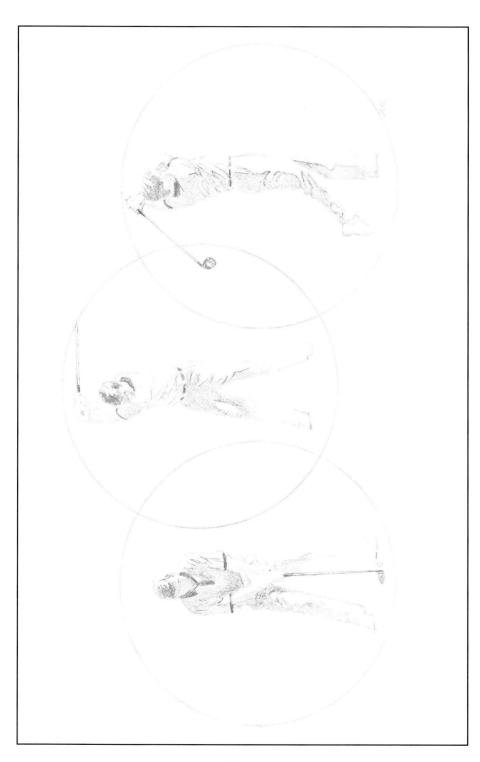

today. Players like Ky Lafoon, Sam Snead, Lloyd Mangrum and Ben Hogan practiced "feel." They concerned themselves with knowing where the clubhead was during the swing. They didn't worry so much about looks. I think that's still the best way.

Today, too many teachers see the golf swing as a sequence of positions. You'll never be able to feel it that way. Try this simple exercise. Get out a sheet of paper and a pen. Now draw a circle. Did you draw it by starting and stopping through a series of arcs? Of course not. If you did, you'll see that it's not a very good circle – it's full of obvious breaks and sure to be a little lopsided. Instead, you just made a single motion and drew a circle on the page. Simple. I want you to think of the golf swing as a circle, and the club as a pen in your hands.

This is why I don't use video when I teach. It's easy to sit down and point out flaws on a video. But it doesn't always help the students. Like a circle, a good golf swing is one continuous motion, back and through. Your mind can't "freeze-frame" in the middle of a swing. If it does, I'll bet the farm that the results won't be very good.

Take a minute and think about all the great athletes in any sport. Have you ever watched Troy Aikman throw a football? Does he make a long, conscious series of movements with his arm? No. He drops back, spots his target, sets his body, and throws the ball with a simple cock and release motion of his arm. Now take a great pitcher like Greg Maddux. He makes a simple wind-up, moving his weight back to his right side and then transferring it to his left and delivering the ball. It's true with any sport. A great boxer throws lightning quick punches because he keeps his preparations simple. Think about how you walk. There's no thought involved. You just take a stride that keeps you in balance, and away you go. That's the way a good golf swing is. You take basic fundamentals and apply them in a simple, well-balanced motion. If you don't get anything else out of this book, I want you to understand that.

Golf isn't a game that you can master. Even the greatest players of all time knew that very early in their careers. That's part of its beauty, though. When the magic settles on you for a day on the golf course, it's like an angel is reaching down from the clouds. What I want you to do is to create the conditions that help the magic happen.

There's a lot more to golf than hitting the ball well and even playing well. Golf is a bond, the center of a community that – as long as you love

the game – you'll always belong to. Hell, I've been teaching for 50 years, and I'll never get tired of seeing students do something that they didn't think they could. Everyone who has ever worked to learn the game understands golf's beauty, difficulty, and the commitment it takes to continue to improve. Watch two golfers – young and old, man and woman, middle handicapper and tour pro – talk about the game. You'll see that the connection goes much deeper than a secret handshake or some crazy lodge greeting. The game brings people together.

Golf has opened so many doors for me. I've gotten to know wonderful people from all around the world. I work with children and senior citizens, and through golf I know that in their hearts people are all the same, no matter how they look or how old they are. If you play golf, the greatest gift that you can give somebody is a love of the game. When you do that, you give a lasting gift that the recipient will never forget. You make yourself a part of the golf community, a chapter in this fantastic story.

In this book I'll share with you some of what I've learned over the last half-century. Not just about the golf swing and the techniques that can help you be a better player, but about the way it's been a part of my life and what golf has helped me do.

We'll spend a little time on the lesson tee and then head out to the course for all kinds of talk about playing this great game, from making the bets on the first tee to managing your game to controlling emotions to having good etiquette so that other people enjoy playing with you. We'll work on practicing so that you can keep on learning by teaching yourself. Finally, we'll sit down at the 19th hole for some of those good times that come when you mix good cheer with good people who love golf.

In these pages I'll share with you some of the stories of the great friends I've made and the places and things I've seen. I hope you can use these observations to enjoy golf more and to help others enjoy it more. That's what it's all about.

It's just that simple.

CHAPTER 2

The Lesson Tee

I've never seen anybody – and that includes Hogan, Nicklaus and Tiger Woods – who was so good at golf that he didn't need any help with his game. The problem is where do you draw the line. I've seen players from beginners to superstars get hooked on teachers. The bottom line is that golf is an individual game. No one can do it for you. Teachers are business people just like all of us. They're looking for repeat business. They'll get you on video and give you a long list of drills that you're supposed to work on between visits. While I believe that most instructors are sincere in wanting to help their students, I see them creating dependencies that end up hurting the golfer in the long run.

Like I said, though, everybody can use a little help. God gave me a gift. I can see the golf swing in very simple terms. I don't care who you are or how well you play, I can spot the one or two big items you should work on in just a few minutes. Then it's up to you. If you let me take longer than 30 minutes with you on the lesson tee, then you're letting me steal your money. The best lessons are simple reminders. They reinforce what you already know, and they break down the complications that creep into your golf game and let you get back to the simple motion of swinging a golf club and making the ball do what you want it to do, no matter how long the shot.

Too many players sign up for lessons and then work on nothing but the long game. In the next several pages we're going to spend a quick session out at the lesson tee. You'll notice that I like to start with the short game and then work up to the long game. That's because the short game breaks golf down to its fundamentals, and that's where all learning begins. It's also because you hit two out of every three shots from inside 60 yards.

Remember, as we work, that you have to judge lessons by what you can take out on the golf course with you. These reminders should get you thinking right. If you can then work on keeping the motions simple, you'll be able to transfer your thinking to the golf course. Here's a good way to judge lessons: If it only works on the range, it's not worth your time or your money.

Short Game Lessons

If you're like most golfers, you rate your game mostly by how good your long shots are. That's the wrong way to look at it. Sure, you'll get a big thrill out of busting a drive 270 yards down the middle, and hitting the ball well is an important part of developing a consistent golf game. But ball striking is messy business. Some days you have the magic, and other days you don't. There's not much difference in a swing that sends the ball soaring on target and one that sends shots just a little bit off line. That's why the short game is so important.

If your golf game had superheroes, the short game would be Clark Kent. At first glance, it's nothing special. After all, we're just talking about short little mild-mannered swings and shots that travel 100 yards or less. But when you're in trouble on the golf course – and everybody gets into trouble out there – your short game becomes Superman, helping you out of tough situations and saving your score on days when your long game just isn't quite right.

I start every lesson with the short game. If you can learn to turn three shots into two, you'll become the best player you can be. The tour pros know this. Look at the stats. Even the very best players average only 12 or 13 greens in regu??tion per round. They know that if they want to get in position to win tournaments, they're going to have to save par with their wedges. And on the days when they're swinging well and hitting the ball straight, those wedges can put them into position for birdies and low scores.

Improving your short game is the fastest and best way to improve your scoring. The more you simplify your approach to getting up and down by using old-fashioned horse sense around the greens, the better your chances of saving your par.

Here are some of my basic tips for improving your short game.

Nick Leason

Define the Target Area

I have an old saying: "Show me a guy who hits it two-feet from the pin all day, and I'll show you a great putter." That's partially true, but the real short game master is the one who can put it two feet away on the proper side of the hole. When preparing to play a short shot, whether it's a chip, a pitch, or a lob, you should have designated a target area that will leave you with the easiest putt to complete the up and down. Generally, this should be below the hole so that you will have a straightforward uphill putt that will allow you to be aggressive.

In order to select the target area, you need to know about the speed, slope, and grain of the greens. These factors will affect the ball once it's on the ground and help you determine the shot with the highest percentage of finding the target area.

Remember, on extremely fast, sloping greens, a two-foot downhill putt may be much more difficult than a five-foot uphill putt. Define your target area accordingly.

Select the Shot

Now that you understand the characteristics of the green and how to define a good target area, you need to select the shot that will give you the best chance of finishing in that target area. There are really only three choices – a chip, a pitch, and a lob.

I advise my students, from bogey golfers to tour players, to keep the ball low to the ground whenever possible. The sooner you can get the ball rolling on the green, the sooner you're on a predictable surface that will accommodate a less than perfect shot. Now that's using the KISS philosophy. Obviously, you have to know all the different shots. If you're in high grass without much green to work with, you can't play the same shot as when you're on hardpan with plenty of green between you and the pin. But you can still find the highest percentage play and use it.

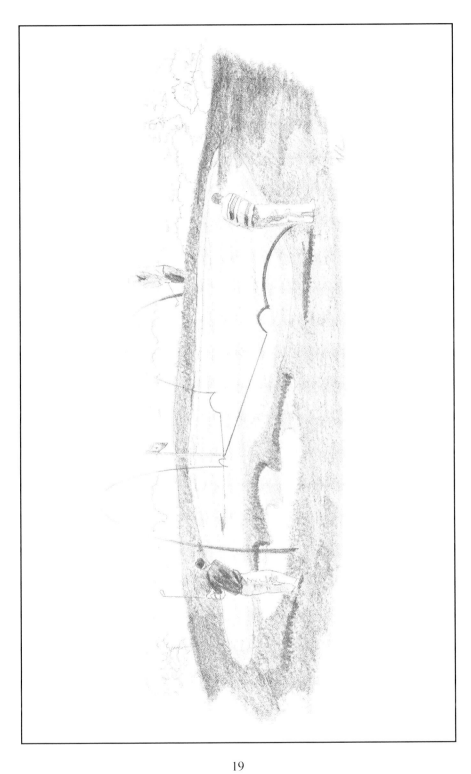

Shot for Each

The most important thing is not to get fancy. Don't try a highlight-film flop shot when a nice little pitch would do the job just as well. Use club selection to help with this. The idea is to use basically the same short game swing for any shot. If you need to hit it higher, take a sand wedge or a lob wedge. You'll get more loft naturally, without having to make major adjustments to your stroke. For more roll, go to a less lofted iron. Sometimes, it's easier to roll a ball up onto the green than to fly it onto the edge with little margin for error. Work backwards from your target area and go with the shot that makes the most sense, not the one that will most impress your playing partners.

The Short Game Stroke

Now it's time to hit the shot. You've already taken a lot of guesswork out of the process, so there's no reason to get complicated when it comes to hitting the ball. If you've got a little shot, make a little shot. The only real goal of the stroke is to hit the ball squarely on the clubface. If you've prepared well, the rest will take care of itself.

The short game stroke is all about tempo and speed. Everybody has a tendency to decelerate, and that's the one thing that will kill an easy short shot. Watch Troy Aikman throw a football. He uses a short, compact passing motion. He doesn't stretch his arm way back and rely on absolutely perfect timing to get rid of the ball properly. That's the way you need to think about the short game stroke. I've never seen anyone hit the ball with the backswing. When you take a long backswing, it means that everything else has to be just perfect, and that's a risk you don't need when trying to get up and down.

My recommendations on the short game stroke are to choke down and take a shorter backswing with the clubhead rarely swinging back beyond knee height. Break your wrists as you take the club away, keeping your right elbow close to your side. Your hands are your most valuable tool when making touch shots.

Make a smooth transition between the backswing and downswing, like walking. When you walk, you just put one foot in front of the other. You don't make a long, complicated motion. That's the rhythm you want on your short shots. Then you just keep your head behind the ball and concentrate on contacting the ball first. There – you've just taken a lot of guesswork out of the short game stroke.

The short game is all mental. The more you can keep it that way, the better your chances of getting up and down every time. Know the greens. Define a target area. Select a shot. And take a simple stroke to play it.

On the Beach

The sand shot is the most misunderstood shot in golf. Watch the tour professionals play from the sand. They almost always give themselves a good up-and-down opportunity from the greenside bunkers. I know players who will actually try to hit their second shots on par-five holes toward a bunker, figuring they have a better shot at birdie from the bunker than they would with a wedge shot from the fairway. But sand still causes most weekend players to get tight and scared, ruining their chances of making a nice, smooth stroke to get out of the bunker and onto the green

There's no reason that you can't hit a sand shot within 10 feet of the hole at least half the time. It's the only shot in golf where you don't even have to hit the ball, for crying out loud. So set aside your anxieties and step into the bunker for a minute.

As with the rest of the short game, the loft of your wedge will determine a lot about the shot. For short bunker shots, use your lob wedge and open the clubface. For longer shots, drop down to your sand wedge. The most difficult bunker shots are the long ones in the 30 and 40-yard range. For these you can fall back to a pitching wedge or even a nine iron. But keep the clubface open. It's much easier to hit a sand shot with an open clubface. An open face helps the clubhead slide through the sand more easily. When the leading edge of a sand wedge hits the sand, it splashes through the sand more than it digs. This effect helps you swing through the ball – the most important key to getting out of the bunker on the first try every time.

Of all the players I've ever seen, no one can handle the bunker shot quite like Gary Player. Watch him play on television. Better yet, get out to a tournament and watch him practice his bunker shots if you get a chance. In the old days, when Player stepped into the practice bunker, he

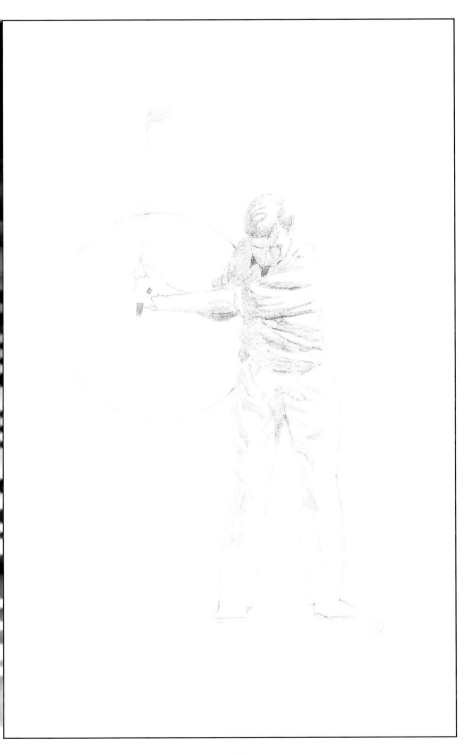

would not come out until he had holed a shot, no matter how long it took. That's one way to improve your sand game.

The beautiful thing about Gary Player's swing from the greenside bunker is how still he stays. That's the key to consistent sand play. Again, choke down on the wedge and open the face appropriately for the length of the shot. Align your feet and body to the left of the target to accommodate the open face.

The swing itself is all arms and hands. Break the wrists early as you swing along the line of your body. Stand tall, and keep your head high throughout the swing. The backswing only goes to about waist high. Remember to keep your right elbow in close to your side for better club control. Now just swing on through the ball, hitting the sand about two inches behind the ball. Let the weight of the clubhead determine the follow through. The ball will just splash right out.

If you start struggling, concentrate on keeping your head still, and if you need a visual aid, lay two quarters behind the ball in the sand and try to hit the back one. You'll be amazed at how easy the sand game can be.

The Putting Green

Putting is the black magic of golf. Ben Hogan said it should be a separate game. Sam Snead would probably agree. On the other hand, Bobby Jones believed that putting should make the difference. All I know is this: The folks who are winning tournaments are the folks who are making putts.

The first thing I'll do to help you become a better putter is to send you back to school for a reading lesson. Reading greens, of course. Most people would make a lot more putts if they had an idea of how the slope and the grain of the green affects the ball. So start your putting lesson by dropping four balls in the center of the putting green and putt the balls to the fringe in all four directions. Notice how the ball behaves differently depending on which direction you're going. The idea is to get a feel for speed. Everybody talks about break, but break is dependent on speed anyway and is a direct result of slope and grain. Until you know how those factors work, you can't figure out the break.

When I talk about grain, I'm talking about how the grass lies. Here

in Oklahoma, where we have a lot of Bent grass greens, the grain can make a huge difference. In general, a putt that goes with the grain will be much faster than one that goes against the grain. Putts that break toward the grain will move more at the end. Putts that break against it will move less. So how can you tell which way the grain is going? Take your foot and lightly scrape the putting surface. If you make the grass stand up, you're scraping against the grain. If it lies down and doesn't resist your scrape, you're going with the grain. The grain tends to lie down toward water and toward the setting sun. Now find yourself some putts that illustrate how the grain affects the ball

Putting is all about tempo. Some teachers say there are two styles of great putters, those who lag the ball into the hole and those who pop it into the back of the hole. I think you need to have a little of both of these styles in your game.

For short putts (10 feet and under), you want to be a little more aggressive. Take a few balls and hit three foot putts at the back of the hole. Focus on a spot at the back of the cup. Make your stroke and then recoil the putterhead back to its original position. This will get you accelerating through the ball.

For longer putts, I like to loosen up my grip a little bit and get a longer stroke going. On these putts it's especially important to play to the line of the putt, not necessarily toward the hole. You want to square up the entire leading edge of the putter to the line that the ball has to start out on. Now make a nice, smooth stroke and don't look up until the ball has rolled out of your peripheral vision.

The other thing I want you to do is develop a good pre-putt routine. Think of a basketball player shooting free throws. He'll bounce the ball the same number of times before each shot. He'll take the same number of breaths. He's making the shooting motion almost automatic. That's how you should approach a putt. Don't make your routine long and involved. It needs to be just long enough to get you in the right mindset to make the stroke.

The putting stroke is all tempo. Your body and head are perfectly still, with the arms and shoulders doing almost all the works. Some putters let their hands work slightly during the stroke. Others keep the hands perfectly still by keeping the wrists firm. Hit a few putts with a few different styles, see what feels right, and then trust it. You'll be fiddling with your putting stroke all your life. Don't be afraid of it.

26

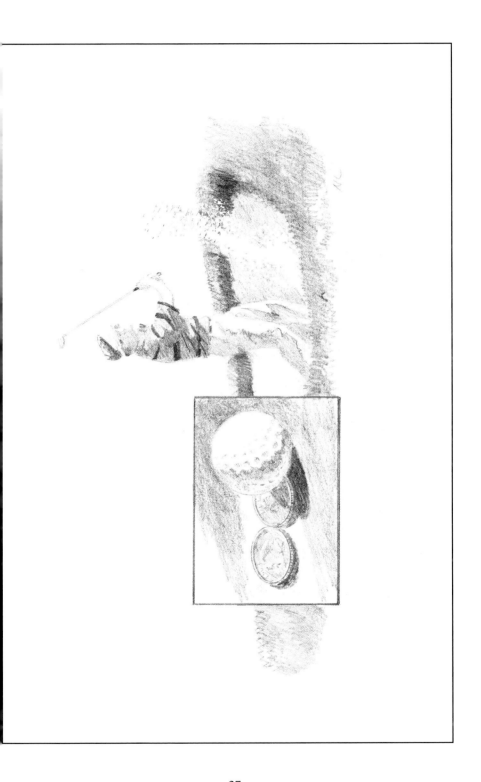

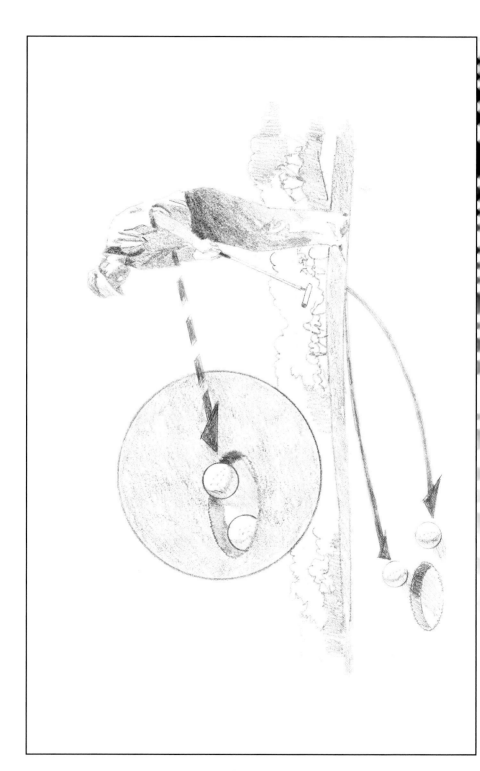

CHAPTER 3

Long Game Lessons

Players who have worked with me know that I believe in hitting the ball long. When you have power, you've got a leg up on the golf course. Your good ball-striking days will give you lots of scoring opportunities. Of course, you have to combine power with a good short game, and we'll spend a lot of time on that in just a little bit. When it comes to excitement, there's nothing that can beat a well-struck full shot.

People always ask me about the best way to introduce their kids to golf. I tell them that you have to teach new players to hit it hard. Hitting the ball hard and square is what hooks new players on golf. Watching the ball fly-off like it might never come down is a thrill that keeps bringing golfers back to the course day after day.

You remember the long hitters. I've seen them all. But the longest hitter I've ever seen was the baseball great Mickey Mantle. Mickey and I were friends for many years, and I'm proud to say that I taught him most of what he knew about playing golf, which ended up being quite a lot. Lord, he could hit it hard. He's the only person ever to drive the green on the 17th hole on the fly at Southern Hills in Tulsa.

Clair Goodwin, sports editor of the Joplin (MO) Globe, once told Mickey that he'd heard the great baseball player could hit a golf ball farther than anybody else alive.

"That's bull," Mickey said. "Who told you that?"

"Marshall Smith said it," Clare told him.

Mickey paused a minute and shook his head. "Well hell, if Marshall told you, then it must be true."

That was a big compliment for me, but it was definitely true about Mickey's power. Not everyone is as strong as Mickey Mantle, that's for sure. But Mickey's secret was in his grip and setup, and that's where you have to start any discussion of the full swing.

The Grip

All great athletes have one thing in common – strong, fast hands. Even in nature, arms and hands are the source of speed. Have you ever watched a hummingbird fly? He beats his wings about 10 times a second, but you don't see him twisting his body into all kinds of contortions to do it. That's what you have to do in golf. If your hands are working correctly, you don't have to belly-whip the ball with your body. Your body simply sets the stage for the hands to release and hit the ball. That means that your grip is crucial to power and consistency because it channels the speed of your hands to the clubhead. A faulty grip hinders the release of the hands and robs you of distance and accuracy.

Most teachers recommend two grips to today's players – overlapping or interlocking. I'm going to teach you another option – and one that I think you should try. But first we'll look at these traditional grips. In both, the left hand position is the same. You hold the club in the bottom three fingers of the left hand, not the palm. Your left thumb should be positioned on top of the shaft, just slightly right of center. This will let the clubhead work properly on the backswing. The right hand positions of the overlapping and interlocking grip are slightly different. In an overlapping, or Vardon, grip, the pinky of your right hand overlaps the index finger of the left hand. In an interlocking grip – famous because it's the one Jack Nicklaus uses – the pinky actually slides underneath the index finger of the left hand.

The idea of both of these grips is to get the hands to work together as a single unit. But for most golfers, I think that's a mistaken goal. Golf is a right-handed game. When I asked my first teacher, the great Ky Lafoon, what he thought about during the swing, he said, "push it back with the left hand, hit the ball with the right." This is good advice. Unfortunately, a lot of golfers put themselves at a big disadvantage by using the two most popular grips. That's why I like to teach the 10-finger, or baseball, grip.

I first noticed the problem with connecting the two hands on the club when I was teaching women, who often have small hands that aren't extremely strong. What I saw was that they never quite released the club all the way. Their shots ended up flying weakly to the right. When I changed them to a baseball grip – the hands in the same position on the

30

lub as with the standard grips but not joined together – the results were mazing.

It doesn't just work for women, either. I'd encourage almost anyone who is learning the game to use the baseball grip, at least in the first couple of seasons. You'll have a better awareness of your hands and how they act during the swing, simply because you have more of your hands in contact with the club. I remember working with the former Heisman Trophy winner Steve Owens. Steve had a sound golf swing but lacked power. Now, there's no reason for a strong man like Steve to have trouble keeping up with the other guys in his group. The biggest change we made was to move him to a baseball grip. Today, Steve's drives are long and straight, and his shots have power and shape; necessary parts of a good golf game.

If you've never tried swinging a club with a baseball grip, you should. Especially if you have trouble leaking the ball to the right or getting the power you think you should have. Don't ever let convention stand in the way of what really works.

The Setup

Once you know how to grip the club properly, you need to know what to do with your body so that your arms and hands can swing freely and generate maximum speed for distance and accuracy. The most simple way of making sure you do that is to master the setup. Way too many golfers worry about what their swing does once it starts. They'd be a lot better off paying attention to what comes before the swing begins. Once the swing begins, it's very difficult to make adjustments.

The setup is the foundation for the golf swing. You wouldn't build a million-dollar house on a sandpit, would you? Of course not, because the ground would not be able to support the weight of the building. Add to that a heavy rainstorm, and your house would soon crumble, ruining all of your hard work. The same is true of the golf swing.

A good player has the clubhead traveling between 85 and 100 miles per hour when it hits the ball. That's a lot of speed. Your body has to be able to control the clubhead at these speeds in order to hit the ball squarely on the clubface and control direction. Once again, a good setup lets you make a simple motion. I like to use the example of a door swinging on its hinges. In a good golf swing, you simply open the door on the way back and close it on the way through the ball. Your body position forms the frame and hinge system that lets you make this simple motion. When it' out of whack, you have to make compensations that are unreliable and usually unsuccessful.

In order to be consistent with your golf swing, you have to stay in balance. If you don't have a good setup, you have no hope of maintaining balance as you swing. You'll move laterally, you'll move up and down all the while changing the angle of the golf club and forcing your body to make unnecesary movements. You'll end up trying to fix something that' not a cause but instead an effect. The KISS approach is to fix the root of the problem. The other things take care of themselves.

You can learn the basics of a good setup without even holding a club in your hands. Imagine that you're on a basketball court, defending your goal. You'll naturally put your feet about shoulder-width apart for balance, with the weight on the insides of your feet, between the ball of the foot and the back of the arch, and your knees just slightly bent. This prepares you to transfer weight in any direction quickly and efficiently Hold your back straight so that you can reach up to deflect a pass over your head.

One of the first things I do with my students is have them set up to the ball. Then I'll come in and just give them a little push with my hand You'd be surprised how easily a 70-year-old man can knock over a stronger younger person. You'd never let that happen in a boxing ring. So why should you let it happen on the golf course?

When you do hold the club and address the ball, remember you dinner manners. Do you slouch over the Sunday table, with your head turned down, away from all your family and friends? No, you don't Instead, you sit up straight and look at the other people at the table. That' the way I want you to set up to the golf ball. When your spine is straight you can easily turn your shoulders around it. By keeping your head up your left shoulder can turn all the way to the ball without having to move your chin out of the way. Remember, a normal head weighs about 1 pounds. That's a lot of weight to be hanging off your spine. Keep you head up and your neck in alignment with the rest of your back.

Now you're ready to try a golf swing.

Swinging the Club

I can't stomach most of the golf instruction on TV and in magazines today. That's because so many instructors are breaking all the movements down so far that there's no way for the golfer to ever get a feel for what is supposed to be happening overall. There are a million ways to deliver the clubhead squarely to the golf ball. But all of those variations share the same simple motion, and you can boil it down to this – push the club back with your left hand and hit through it with your right hand. You can talk all you want about pronating the wrists and matching the angles of the clubface and hands and shoulders and whatnot, but all that really matters is that you get the club moving back and through in a simple, continuous motion. If you've worked on the grip and setup fundamentals we've already discussed, things will take care of themselves. Just get behind the ball, keep your right elbow in close to your side, and swing away.

Same Swing, Different Shots

Now, people ask me all the time about using one swing for all clubs or different swings for different clubs. I'll just tell you this – there's only one swing, and you either make a full swing or a partial version of that same swing. For instance, it doesn't make sense to try to hit a seven iron the same way you'd hit a driver. But the swing is the same, just a little shorter and a little slower. Common sense, right?

We'll talk later about specialty shots – how to hit the ball high or low, make it curve to the left or right. But the source of all those shots is the same. If you can learn to make a simple, powerful swing that brings together the basics of grip, setup, and rhythm, you can play this game.

Practice That Works

We've just finished going over some lessons that can make a real difference in your golf game – if you can bring them to the golf course. That's where practice comes in. People will tell you that practice makes perfect. I'll tell you that this old saying isn't always true when it comes to golf. Good practice makes improvement. That's how I'd write it up. You practice in order to hone skills that you can use on the golf course. That means you have to treat practice with the same seriousness and high regard that you treat a round of golf.

I think practicing is one of the most misunderstood parts of golf. Think of how often you've heard a friend – or maybe even yourself – say, "I'm going out to hit some balls." Show me a guy who goes to the range to "hit some balls," and I'll show you a guy who won't ever get it right on the course. That's because he hasn't learned the right way to practice.

I've been lucky. When I was young my good friend George Coleman had a visitor from Texas come stay with him in my hometown of Miami, Oklahoma. The friend was one of his fellow professionals, a small, quiet man named Ben Hogan. You can make the argument that Ben Hogan was one of the best golfers ever to play the game. But there's no doubt that he was the very best who ever lived when it came to practicing.

Hogan practiced with the same famous intensity he showed on the course. He was hard on himself, a perfectionist who judged every shot – even on the range – as though his career hung on its outcome.

"Mr. Hogan," someone once asked, "when you're practicing, how often are you working on something specific and how often are you simply grooving your swing?"

Hogan answered with a characteristic snort. "I'm always working on something specific," he said, "Or I wouldn't be here."

On several occasions in 1947 I got to shag balls for Mr. Hogan. Fifty years later, I can still see those shots coming at me. It's a shame that

kids don't get the chance to shag balls these days. There's no better way to learn about shotmaking than to see it from the receiving end. Driving ranges have become big business, and automatic ball pickers have ended the great tradition of shagging balls, just like golf carts have all but done away with caddies. But I'll never forget what it was like to be stationed at exactly 145 or 163 or 187 yards from Hogan and his mountain of balls. And when I say exactly, I mean it. If I had to take a step forward or back to catch the shot, Hogan would shake his head in disgust – not at the inaccuracy of his ball striking but at the inaccuracy of my paces. The thing I'll always remember is the shape of those shots. He would hit high ones that I'd play like pop flies. Then he'd hit low ones that came screaming at my mitt like extra-base line drives. He'd bend shots from right to left. Then from left to right. And never did I have to move to field the ball. I can't tell you how much I learned on those hot afternoons. It's one thing to stand on the tee firing shots at a pin. It's quite another to be the pin.

There are so many lessons in Hogan's practice technique, but the one that has stuck with me the longest, as player and teacher, is his devotion to precision. He was never trying to see how far he could hit the ball. Instead, he was always trying to hit it exactly so far. Whether it was a driver, a wedge, a five-iron, it didn't matter. The object was to hit the precise shot he imagined. Anything less was failure. In other words, Ben Hogan never once went to the practice range to "hit balls." He was there to hit shots. I suggest you take a cue from the master on that point.

How much should you practice? That's a personal choice. I've known players who would practice four times a week and only play once. That seems a little backwards to me, but then I've always enjoyed playing golf more than practicing. I guess the only real guideline is that you should practice enough to show improvement on the course. If you spend your practice time wisely – rehearsing for the shots you'll have to hit when you play – you'll find that you don't need endless hours of range work. If you just go out and start swinging away on the practice tee, then no amount of work will be enough. It will never result in lower scores.

If you want to improve your play through practice, you're going to have to make your practice work for you.

Focus on the Short Game

The biggest problem people have with practicing is that they've got the percentages all wrong. They go out and hit hundreds of full shots and totally ignore the most important part of scoring – the short game. We've all seen so-called short-game magicians. Seve Ballesteros is one. So is Tom Kite. You probably know someone at your home course who never seems to have a horrible score, even when he's hitting it badly. Don't think that these guys were just born with great imagination and soft hands. I know better. I've seen some of the greatest short game players of all time, and I'll tell you this: not a single one of them was born with it. They had to develop their skills the old-fashioned way, by practicing. This is good news for you.

Gary Player is the greatest bunker player of all time. A lot of golfers know that. What they don't know is that Gary used to go into the practice bunker every day and not leave until he had holed out a shot. If he holed out the first one, that was it. But if it took eight hours, he would stay in there until a shot found the cup. The point of this story is that every time he hit a practice shot, he was trying to make it. That carried over into his on-course game, and the rest is history. In other words, he practiced with on-course performance in mind, and it paid off.

The fact is that more than half of the shots you hit on the course measure 60 yards or less. Knowing what to do around the greens can wash away many of the sins your full swing commits. It's just a simple matter of math that you should be spending about 70-75% of your practice time on pitching, chipping, bunker play and putting. This is the fastest way to see practice make a difference in your scores. It's All in the Mix

The short game is all about distance control and understanding how the ball will behave once it is on the green. You can hit high lob shots that hardly run at all, or you can go for low shots that spend most of their time rolling. Practicing the short game is the only way to get a feel for proper shot selection, and that's what lets you save strokes. Stand in the same place with five balls and hit five different shots to the same target. What are the advantages, or disadvantages of each? Your opponents may start talking about your "imagination" on the course. You'll know it's just plain old common sense.

On the course, no two short shots are alike. That's the way it should be in your practice sessions as well. You need to practice all types of shots from all types of lies. Work your way around the practice green in a big circle, hitting a few shots from 20-10- 5 yards from the green's edge. Work off of downhill, sidehill and uphill lies and make a mental note of how your stance and lie affect the shot. When you go into the bunker, practice shots from good lies, from footprints, from rake grooves. Bury balls up under the lip and figure out the most effective way to get out. Practice long shots and short ones.

The goal of short game practice is to eliminate "surprises" on the course. Major league batters know that a pitcher is most effective during his first rotation through the order. After that, you've seen his windup, delivery and the movement of the pitches. There's no real surprise, and the hitters begin to feel more comfortable. Your short game practice should let you know what kind of shots the course can throw at you. If you've seen it before, it's just not as intimidating.

A Little Help from Your Friends

The best thing you can do for short game practice is to invite a friend to join you. I used to get into tremendous practice green games with former PGA Tour player Woody Blackburn. We would challenge each other at a dollar a shot; winner of the last shot gets to pick the next. We ended up playing all types of up-and-down shots – over hedges and trees, under branches, shots that had to roll through bunkers, you name it. And there's no better putting practice than playing small-stakes games on the putting green. What I love about this kind of competitive practicing is that it helps you keep your focus and teaches you to deal with the pressure you're sure to encounter when you're playing. And there's nothing better than "putting a needle," i.e. sticking it to a friend, even if it's just for some tees or a Coke. Practice that stokes your competitive fires is practice that will stay with you for a long, long time, especially if it's practice that teaches you how to save strokes.

Home on the Range

Now, I'm not against full-swing practice. You need it in order to become a better ball-striker. What I'm against is the idea of going out just

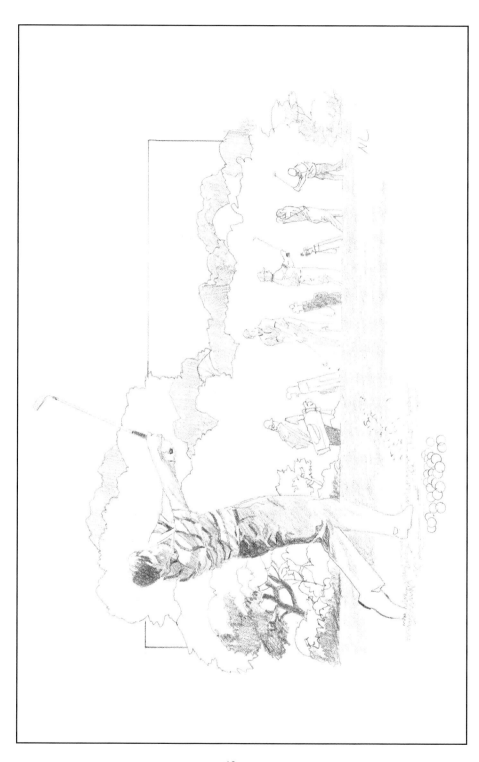

to pound balls into a wide open driving range. Practice is a discipline. There's no other word for it. In many areas of life today, discipline is in short supply. But if you want to improve your golf game and put yourself in a better position to enjoy all the benefits this great game can deliver, discipline is key. There's an old Chinese saying: "A mule is good if tamed, but he who tames himself is better ." That's what practicing is all about, taming yourself. That's why you need to have a consistent and manageable practice routine.

A good practice routine helps you focus on the session and block out other distractions. One of my favorite photographs shows a golfer intently practicing on the range while the clubhouse is literally in flames behind him. The message is clear – his practice routine had begun, and nothing was going to snap him out of it.

Your practice session should always begin with goal-setting. What do you plan to carry away from the range on that particular day? Write it down before you begin. Be specific with both your long game and short game. For instance, you may want to work on drawing the ball with your mid-irons. Or you may want to work on trajectory – getting a higher or lower ball flight. Maybe you've been struggling with the soft lob shot. Don't set goals that you can't achieve. If you consistently hit a severe left-to-right banana ball, you're not going to start drawing it in one session. In that case you might want to focus on turning that sharp slice into a fade that you can play. But always have goals and commit to them.

Once your goals for the session are clear, take the time to warm up properly so that your body and mind are ready to get down to business. Start by selecting your practice location. By that I mean where on the range you are going to work. I have my students work at one end of the range, as far away from other people as possible. The range is no place for socializing. You want to be able to concentrate and work, like an artist in a studio.

Take your sand wedge and start by hitting a few 20-yard shots. Work on making simple swings, feeling your hands and arms working while minimizing body movement. When you're comfortable at 20 yards, move to 50-yard shots. Hit a few of those, again making nice, even-tempo swings and concentrating on solid contact in the middle of the clubface. Think about rhythm – back and through. Point your thumb to heaven on the backswing, and shake hands with your friend on the follow-through.

Once you feel loose and limber, it's time to move on into the meat of the session.

Work your way through the bag, starting with your sand wedge and then moving to the longer clubs. I like to go through all the even numbered clubs in one session and then the odd numbered clubs in the next. This way, you're sure to work with all the clubs in your bag, building confidence and reducing the idea of having "favorite" clubs.

The practice tee is the place to work on fundamentals. Tempo is the most important element of any golf swing. Sing to yourself to establish a tempo and swing in time. You may want to lay clubs down along the line of your stance and the ball to improve alignment. Keep your grip pressure light and go through your pre-shot routine before each shot. Pay attention to your grip, posture, setup and ball position. The practice tee is no place to rush through a big bag of balls. Remember, you're there to hit shots, not balls.

When practicing, you should always value accuracy over distance. Select small targets to encourage precise shotmaking. One of the best practice sessions I ever saw came during a Senior Tour event, when I was working with Chi-Chi Rodriguez and Walt Zembriski. Off in the distance a turtle was making his way across the range. For more than an hour I had Chi-Chi and Walt hitting shots at that turtle. On every shot the target was just slightly different, but it was always small. Think about it. When you've been standing there aiming at a turtle, a green is going to look pretty big. The lesson for you is to pick the smallest target you can find – and don't let it get away.

A practice session is full of great opportunities to improve skills that will make you a better player, and it's not always swing skills that you should work on. Distance control is a perfect example. When you stand out on the tee hitting balls, you're not paying a lot of attention to exactly how far the balls travel. You should be. I make all of my students pace off shots so that they'll know exactly how far they're trying to hit. Then I make them pace off the distance between where the ball ends up and the target.

Thanks to sprinkler heads, fairway plates and yardage books, golfers almost always know the precise distance to the target when they're on the course. That won't do you any good, though, if you don't know how far you hit the ball with each club. Start pacing when you practice. If

the range is busy and you can't actually pace off your shots, you should at least pace off the distance between measurement plates and the tee markers. Your practice sessions should leave you knowing exactly how far you hit each club, from your lob wedge to your driver. If you get nothing out of practicing except that knowledge, then you've spent your time wisely.

The Only Drills You'll Ever Need ...

A lot of players – from amateurs to touring pros – have asked me for drills they can use on the range. I'm not a big believer in complex drills. Most of the time you can't use them on the golf course anyway. But there are a couple of drills that I like to incorporate into every practice session, usually after I've finished working through all my clubs. The first is the "half-swing" drill. Take 20 balls and hit them using only half swings. The club should point up to the sky on the backswing and up to the sky again on the follow-through.

The second drill is similar to the first but adds to it. This is the "one club, many targets" drill. Take a club, say a 7-iron, and hit five balls to a target at normal 7-iron distance (about 150 yards for most golfers). Then hit five balls to a target 10 yards nearer than the first. Then five more to a target another 10 yards nearer, all the way down to about 100 yards. This teaches you to scale your swing while maintaining good rhythm. Work on staying behind the ball and accelerating through the shot, regardless of how long it is. Both of these drills help you to focus on hitting the ball square while making nice, controlled swings.

...And a Surprise Ending for Your Range Session

You've now constructed a good practice routine, but your range session isn't quite finished yet. With the last 10 balls of the day I want you to think back to the most difficult, awkward, full shots you faced the last time you played. You may have had to hit a ball under low-hanging branches, or you may have needed to bend a shot around a tree or into a crosswind. You may have encountered a shot off hardpan or out of a divot. The hardest shots to hit are the ones you've never tried. And again, if the goal of practice is to improve your on-course play, then you need to keep the course at the front of your mind during practice. Ending your session

this way will help. Recall those difficult shots and recreate them on the range. Hit each of the two shots five times, experimenting to gain a feel for what will be successful in dealing with the situation. These are lessons that you give yourself. Soon enough, you will come to understand that your own practice may be the greatest teacher of all.

Practicing on the Golf Course

You play golf on the golf course, not on the driving range. So the best place to practice would obviously be on the course itself, right? The range can be a good substitute, but you should never pass up the opportunity to get some of what I call "live" practice. Try to get out in the early morning or late afternoon when you will not be slowing traffic or disturbing other players. Even three or four holes of on-course practice can be a real boost for your game.

My favorite way to practice on the course is to play two balls. Play each hole two different ways. On a dogleg, you may want to play one ball with a driver, cutting off distance and going for birdie. Take the conservative route with the other ball. You'll soon get a feeling for percentages and for the style that makes you most comfortable.

Another great practice game is to tee off on every hole with a 5-iron. That way, you'll end up hitting approach shots with clubs you would never normally hit. Anything that can extend and challenge your comfort zone is good for your game. If you've had trouble with a certain hole because you tend to miss the ball to the right, spend some time in your trouble spot. Practice different escape shots from different positions in the right rough so that you'll be prepared the next time you're forced to play out of that area. Then go back and try to play the hole a different way, with another iron off the tee for instance. You just might find that you've been trying to force a square peg into a round hole rather than playing to your strengths. Those kinds of discoveries are what good practice is all about.

Think about this question: What have your last five practice sessions taught you about your game? If you have trouble coming up with an answer, you need to overhaul your practice strategy. Good luck!

CHAPTER 5

The Golf Course

There are a lot of great games in the world. I've loved baseball and football all my life. I'm sure that I could learn to love soccer, cricket, rugby or tennis. But golf is the greatest game of all. And one of the greatest things about the game is that we play it on golf courses. No two golf courses are alike. They don't rest on the land. They are the land. Golf courses change with the seasons. They recede in the Fall as the color fades from the fairways and the trees, and they emerge in the Spring. Think of how you feel when you see the green grass returning. Golf courses mature with age. Trees grow and change the strategies of certain holes. When a famed tree dies – it happened at Winged Foot recently when a beautiful, historic tree behind the ninth green had to be removed – the members may actually mourn the loss. These qualities make golf courses the most magnificent sporting venues on earth, places capable of inspiring a quiet reverence or a thrilling sense of exhiliration. When I look back on my life in golf, I remember the golf courses just as I remember the faces of all the friends I've made in the game.

Golfers spend too much energy trying to master the particulars of the golf swing, the putting stroke or the other technical parts of the game. I think you should start your search for lower scores by simply loving the golf course. When you're on the course, you're spending quality time with your friends and family in a beautiful setting. You're doing something you love to do. If there's one mistake I see people make over and over, it's that they treat golf like work. We call it "playing" golf for a reason. Don't get me wrong. Any time you commit yourself to anything, you should take it seriously and try to do it as well as you can. But golf isn't a matter of life and death. It's only a matter of life and of living.

I say a little prayer of thanks every time I step onto the first tee, and you should, too. Golf is a gift. And the golf course is the wrapping. Think of how you feel when you receive a present. It's not always what's inside the box that matters, it's the spirit of the moment. I want you to see golf as a celebration and a search for beauty, not a quest for perfection.

Take Refuge on the Golf Course

We live most of our lives on concrete. That's where we work, where we drive, where we do our hectic thinking and planning. If you love golf, the golf course is your refuge from all of that. I knew Mickey Mantle practically his whole life. Only on the golf course did he ever truly relax. You could see the tension drain out of him as soon as he stepped onto the first tee. On the course, you know that you will get the space to pursue your game without all the interruptions of the concrete world. You're a member of a global club.

I've never understood why people put so much pressure on themselves to perform. You don't put pressure on yourself to enjoy the beach or to savor a quiet evening in the mountains. You just feed off the beauty of the environment. Performance in golf comes from feeling that you're an extension of the golf course. All you have to do is move that little ball around from place to place. You're going to have a bad round every now and then. You need to ask yourself some hard questions if you let a bad round turn into a bad day. Walter Hagen said to "stop and smell the flowers." What he meant was that you shouldn't put so much pressure on your game. Imagine a golf course in the early morning. The dew is shining in the sunlight. You smell the freshly cut grass. The birds are singing all around you, and the people who are with you are there because they share your love of the game. If you can't sit at your desk and feel more peaceful with those images, then you should find another pastime. Now why should you block all of that out by thinking of nothing but your golf game when you arrive at the course?

I've played hundreds of golf courses in my life, and I've found something to love about every one of them. It's an honor to play a fine golf course. You get to walk on history. You can't go play catch at Yankee Stadium, but I played the West Course at Winged Foot just after Davis Love III won the PGA Championship there. As I came up to the final hole, I couldn't help but imagine how Davis must have felt only a few days before. I thought of Davis and how proud his late father, a famous golf instructor I knew quite well, must have been, watching from the clouds.

I thought about the rainbow that appeared as Davis raised his arms in his first major championship victory, and it gave me the shivers. Golf is unique among all sports in that it gives you the chance to test your own game on the very same courses that decide the most famous tournaments in the world.

Of course, you'll strike history at any golf course if you dig a little. When I was younger I used to play a lot of golf at Baxter Springs Golf Club in Baxter Springs, Kansas. The course is only nine holes and will never host a U.S. Open or be featured in a Golf Digest ranking, but I witnessed history there. In those days the greens at Baxter Springs were sand greens with an oil base. You actually had to run a drag across the line of your putt to smooth out the surface. I often played there with a very good friend of mine who was a member, and sometimes his young son would join us for a few holes. I was so impressed with the youngster's swing and natural understanding of the game that on one of my visits to Baxter Springs I brought him a set of four cut-down clubs. Little did I know that I would later see that same boy win three U.S. Open titles (including one at Winged Foot). His name was Hale Irwin.

Find the Beauty

History, tradition, and natural setting come together in a golf course as they do nowhere else. When people ask me about my favorite courses I have to stop and think. There's nothing more beautiful than seaside golf. The ocean stretches out forever, and there you are, playing on the edge of the world. Mountain golf can take your breath away with its scenic views. Then again, you could never beat the beauty of our own little club here in Miami, Oklahoma. The trees and the wind that blows in from the plains are sweet music for sure, and should you post an under-par score, the club members will have you sign Doctor W.D. Jackson's old hat that hangs in the bag room. You then become a part of the history and tradition of our club. Well, you get the picture. If you look for the beauty in any golf course, you'll find it. And when you find it, you've done more for your game than any amount of lessons could ever do. You've put things in perspective.

My favorite story of finding the beauty of a golf course is the story of Bobby Jones and his first visit to Saint Andrews. Bobby Jones was just a teenager – obsessed as all teenagers are with trying to control his surroundings – when he visited the Old Course for the first time. There, the future king of the game encountered a landscape and course design he had never seen. To say that he failed to appreciate it at first would be an understatement. In fact, in his first competitve round, he got caught in a pot bunker and rather than take his medicine and play out sideways, he chose to flail away in an unsuccessful attempt to advance the ball. After posting a double-digit number on the hole he stormed off the course and back to the clubhouse. There he received a warning, in no uncertain terms, that such behavior would not be tolerated ever again in a Royal & Ancient competition. That incident did more to make Jones a complete player than anything else in his career. He learned to stop fighting the golf course and start learning how to play it as it was. Jones returned to win an Open Championship on the storied links of Saint Andrews, and in his later years he often remarked that if he could play only one course for the rest of his life, Saint Andrews would be his choice. He found the beauty of the golf course, and it made him a better player.

Finding the beauty of a golf course sometimes means letting go of your ego. One of the most common sources of frustration that I see among golfers is that they don't play the course as it's meant to be played. Usually it's because they don't play the proper set of tees. Why on earth would an 18-handicapper want to ever play a course from the championship tees? It's very hard to find beauty when you spend all your time looking for balls because you can't reach the fairway from the tee. Select the tees that the architect meant for golfers of your skill level. Then play the course to the best of your ability. You'll have more fun, you'll find more beauty and you'll play better golf.

Do Your Part

In order to find beauty on the golf course, you need to respect beauty. Keeping a golf course in good condition requires a lot of work. Just ask any superintendent. We've come to expect our golf courses to be just about perfect, but that perfection doesn't happen overnight. You'd be shocked to see how early the grounds crew gets started every morning just so you will have a well-manicured course to enjoy. That's why you have to pitch in by making sure that you leave the golf course in the same great shape in which you found it, if not better. Some people call this "responsibility." I call it common courtesy toward your fellow golfers, and it's just as important as the etiquette of playing golf.

I don't think there's anything more pathetic than a beautiful putting surface covered with ball marks. If you're fortunate enough to make a ball mark, that means you're usually right around the green. To get to repair a ball mark is an achievement that you can savor and enjoy. Watch the pros on tour. They make a ritual of repairing their pitch marks. You should, too. Always carry a ball mark tool, or better yet collect them from every course you play so that you'll always have some extras in case you notice that someone in your group is without one. Then make sure you repair the pitch mark correctly by digging in at the edges and pulling the meat of the mark toward the front. The idea is to lay the grass back over the ball mark so that the repaired mark is unobtrusive. If you start in the center of the mark and dig too deeply, you'll simply pull sand up from underneath the roots of the grass, and then you've only made the problem worse. If you have holed out and are waiting for other players to finish putting, repair another mark or two off to the side so that you've left the green in even better condition than you found it.

You can also do your part to eliminate spike marks. If you haven't already done so, get your shoes equipped with softspikes. If you're worried about balance during the swing, then you're swinging too hard anyway. Many courses require spikeless alternatives (there are a number of brands), and more are joining the list every day. If you insist on steel spikes, you're fighting a losing battle. Spikeless shoes can go a long way toward improving putting surfaces all over the country, but you can still do damage if you don't bother to lift your feet when you walk. The old advice to "walk like you're going somewhere" certainly applies here. You'll be doing a service to everyone on the course.

Be sure and replace your divots in the fairway. If the course you're playing provides a dirt/seed mixture, use it. Otherwise, take the few seconds and collect your divot, replacing it properly by aligning the grain of the grass on the divot to the grain of the fairway. It surely won't take you long to start cursing other golfers when you hit a perfect drive that ends up smack in the middle of a deep divot. Don't let yourself be the target of someone else's curses.

Obey the cart path rules, even when you don't understand them. If there's a "cart path only" rule or a "90-degree" rule, it's because the superintendent is trying to protect the fairway from damage due to the weight of the cart. Always put the good of the golf course above your own personal convenience. Besides, if you're young and healthy you should be walking the course anyway!

Finally, learn how to rake the bunkers. Would you trust a person who didn't clean up his mess in the kitchen before you came to start cooking? Of course not. It's just as rude on the golf course to leave a bunker unraked. The players behind you don't want to be playing out of your footprints or sand divots. All it takes is a couple of seconds to smooth out the sand's surface so that your fellow golfers will have a chance to get up and down.

If you already follow these course maintenance guidelines, see if there are ways that you could do them better. And always help teach new players – and careless veterans – the importance. You belong to the community of golfers, and your golf course reflects on that community. Show a little pride in it.

CHAPTER 6

Course Management

Every round of golf you play is the culmination of all the lessons and practice you've ever put into your game. That's one of the most beautiful things about the sport – you never stop learning. And golf is the greatest teacher of all. Golf reveals and strengthens character. Grantland Rice, the great sportswriter, always said that you could learn more about a person in 18 holes of golf than you could in 18 years of sitting across a desk. Golf tests your nerves and your composure. It highlights both your best and worst qualities.

I've been playing golf for more than 65 years, and I've had the great fortune to play with some of the very best golfers in history. And I can tell you this – not one of them has ever mastered the game. Ky Lafoon used to tell me that one man had mastered it but he was in the state hospital. If you know golf, you know what he means. The great Ben Hogan told me that he was lucky to hit a half-dozen shots in a round that came off the way he imagined them. Jack Nicklaus, the most prolific winner of all time, played himself into contention time and again not by out-performing the field but by limiting his mistakes. In other words, he accepted that he was going to make mistakes. He just tried to make fewer of them than anyone else. Care to argue with his strategy? He made it simple.

You may wonder why I'm telling you all of this. It's because too many amateurs – and professionals as well – seem to think that mastering the game is their goal. Golf isn't about how many great shots you hit. It's about how good your bad shots are. It's about the power to accept your limitations, to recover from your errors and to use faith, hope and love so that you're always looking to the promise in your next shot. It sounds an awful lot like life when you start to think of it that way.

In this section I want to talk to you about how to get the most from your game on the golf course. You don't have to be a scratch player to feel the joy of setting a personal best – or to feel the pain of letting a great round slip away. You just have to be human, and you have to care. I've played with tour players and with raw beginners, and I know that it's the same thing that brings both of them back the next time. It's the possibility that today is going to be your day. And if you manage the course well, it just may be.

Stay In Control

You've probably heard the term "course management," but do you really know what it means? Basically, course management is matching the resources of your game to the demands of the golf course. Most people create their own problems, on the golf course or anywhere else. If you pay attention to the patterns of your game and the design of the golf course, you should be able to negotiate your way around the trouble and shoot a good score, even on days when your swing isn't quite right.

If you study all the great players, you will see that they all know you don't have to hit perfect shots to play well . You have to manage the course well. I remember when Craig Stadler played in the 1994 PGA Championship at Southern Hills in Tulsa. The first day he hit seven greens but shot 70. The second day he hit only four greens and shot another 70. The third day he struck the ball beautifully and hit 13 greens. I'll give you one guess what his score was. That's right, another 70. Don't depend on great ball-striking for good scoring. Manage your game.

Chi-Chi Rodriguez and Hale Irwin are two of the finest players I've ever seen at keeping the wheels from falling off. The reason is that they play one shot at a time without letting the frustration build up to a breaking point. They trust their short games, and they stay patient and wait for their scoring opportunities. Another player who can salvage a good round on an off day is Greg Norman. I remember when the U.S. Open was at Shinnecock Hills a few years ago. In the third round Norman hit only four greens in regulation, yet he still shot 70 and stayed in contention. Anybody can have a lucky day, but the better you are at course management, the luckier you'll get. The absolute best exercise you can do for improving your decision making skills is to pay attention to the golf you watch on television. Resist the temptation to be overwhelmed by the distance the pros get on their shots or the number of birdies they make.

That's impressive, all right, but it's not how they make their money. The way they make their money is to miss the shot in the right spot, leaving themselves good up-and-down opportunities, and they don't throw away shots on foolish gambles. They know where the trouble is, and they play away from it. Then they play aggressively when a hole suits their games.

One good strategy is to think about making pars, not miracles. A bogey will never kill you. All it takes is one birdie to wipe it out. But double-bogeys and worse will do you in, whether you're playing for a major title or a friendly Nassau. And remember that most double-bogeys are the resultsof a concentration lapse, not a series of poorly executed shots. Here are some of the ways you can improve your course management. These are the same methods the top professionals use, and if they seem a little simple, it's because they are. If you're looking for magic, go find a magician. Wisdom is usually right there between your ears, trying to get out.

Get Off on the Right Foot

A good, solid beginning to a round is the surest way to gain confidence that will carry you through the day. So many players are scared to play well. They don't think they're capable of it. I'll bet you know someone who consistently starts off poorly and then pours it on the rest of the way. If he could get off to a good start, he'd shave three or four shots from his round and quickly lower his handicap and develop a more consistent game. The reason for this pattern is that he isn't comfortable being at even par. He's comfortable being three or four over par. Psychologically, that's when he starts playing well. I'm here to tell you that you should never wait for disaster. Take control of your game from the very first shot.

Start with a good warm-up. Notice that I didn't say a "full" or "complete" warm-up. I said a good one. That means a warm-up that prepares you to play the first hole. Golf takes a lot of time, so most players don't arrive at the course until just a few minutes before their tee time. The worst thing you can do if you're cutting it close on time is to run out on the range to make full swings. Your warm-up should focus almost exclusively on balance and tempo. And what's the best way to do that? With simple little short shots. I'd rather see you over at the practice green hitting 10 little chips and pitches, working to keep your body nice and quiet, using your hands and arms in nice, rhythmic swings that let you feel the balance in your feet. Then you can stretch your body by making a few full swings without even hitting a ball. Just keep that same tempo and balance and take four or five swings. Finally, head over to the putting green. Hit a few lag putts to get a feel for distance control and a few three-foot putts, and you've done about all the warming-up you need to do. It shouldn't take you any more than 10 minutes. The last thing you want to do is show up at the first tee tired and anxious because you didn't give your body and mind a decent chance to adjust to the rhythm of the game.

Set Your Own Goals

If we had softball tryouts and put you up against a major-league pitcher, you would end up looking – and feeling – pretty silly. But that's what too many golfers do when they judge their game against the par on the scorecard. Par is always a great target on any hole, but it's an unreasonable standard for a 10-handicapper. Likewise, if you're an aspiring tour pro, shooting par won't make you much money. I make all my students set their own targets for a golf course. Have you ever noticed yourself getting stuck on a score? It can get to the point that you shoot that score – maybe it's 72 or 77 or 89 – no matter how well or poorly you play. Most people respond by tightening up and trying even harder to improve against par when the right answer would be to set that score as a target and just try to beat it by one shot. Pick a par that's right for you. Then go out and break it. The par on the scorecard is only one way of goal-setting.

First Tee Jitters

The first tee strikes fear in the heart of a lot of golfers. That just doesn't make sense to me. You're not trying to do anything you've never done before. All you have to do is put the ball in play, and you're off to the races. But somehow, it gets turned into this big, nervous production. You start gripping the club too tightly and make a tense, fast swing that is probably the worst of the day. If you've warmed up properly, you'll feel relaxed and ready. You won't be trying to guide the ball, the greatest sin of all on the first tee. Instead, you'll be able to make a nice, aggressive swing with a full release and good acceleration through the ball. Try to steer the ball off the first tee, and you'll drive yourself right into trouble.

Once you are past that first tee shot, establish the tone of the round. If you're going to try a risky shot, don't do it early. A string of pars, at the start of a round, will always get you into the right frame of mind.

Know Your Game

When you were driving to the course, you were – hopefully – careful to obey to traffic signals on the road. When there's a red light you don't just fly through the intersection and hope for the best. You stop. A yellow light could mean stop or go, but you took the time to analyze the situation and make a smart decision. Even when the light is green, you make sure that there are no unexpected dangers before continuing through the intersection. Your golf game will give you signals just as obvious as traffic lights if you pay attention to them. If you obey these signals, you're playing percentage golf, and percentage golf is good golf.

Unlike traffic lights, your on-course signals will vary from day to day. I'm sure you've heard television announcers talk about how particular holes set up well for particular players. Take Craig Stadler, for instance. Craig tends to play a left-to-right shot. Pins that are tucked on the left side, behind bunkers and near trouble, would normally pose a problem for him. But like all golfers, Craig's game varies from round to round. There's an old saying that you have to "dance with the person you brought." If you normally hit a fade but are hitting a draw on a certain day, then use that draw to fire at pins you might otherwise avoid. A golf course is made up of 18 birdie opportunities. If you're not hitting the ball well, or if a hole doesn't set up for the shot you're hitting that day, play to the middle of the green, make your par and get out of there.

Beware of the "sucker pin." I don't care how good you are, there are some shots you just shouldn't try. Always make a note of the margin of error on every shot you plan to hit. When a pin is close to the side of an elevated green, a shot that just misses by a few feet can carom off the side of the hill and put you in big trouble. Think back to the short game lessons at the beginning of the book. Your target area isn't a big circle – it's more like a teardrop, with the small end of the drop being the hole and the target extending out in a larger shape to one side of the hole. Green lights become easier to see, and so do red lights. Now you're giving yourself a chance to play smart golf. Managing the course puts you in position to take advantage of your good breaks without having to rely on them.

Too many golfers get impatient. They try to overpower the golf course, and they end up making bad decisions that cost them big numbers. Be aware of the golf course, then just think about tempo and swing the club. If you have to think about scores, think about this: Make par on all the par-three holes and birdie on all the par-five holes. If you do that you'll have a great round.

Anger

I'm not going to get up on a soapbox about anger. You're just not human if you don't get a little upset at bad swings and stupid mistakes. My good friend and teacher Ky Lafoon, one of the very best players I've ever known in my life, had a fierce temper, and it cost him a number of tournament victories. Tommy Bolt could have been one of golf's greatest, but he let his temper hold him back. No one remembers Tommy Bolt's magnificent play when he won the U.S. Open at Southern Hills. Instead, they will remember forever the famous photograph of Tommy hurlng his driver into the lake on the finishing hole at Cherry Hills in Denver. Is that how you want your partners to remember you?

You have to keep a clear mind in order to play good golf. Your temper is a mish-mash of emotions. It's part pride, part arrogance and part desire. You can let these emotions work against you, or you can learn to put them to work for you. Almost everyone who has taken up golf has had to put the reins on his temper, eventually. If you don't, it can get ugly. The other people in your group have to accommodate your attitude. Soon, they'll get tired of doing it, and you'll have trouble finding a game. On top of that, flying clubs are dangerous weapons. What makes you think you can throw a club accurately if you can't hit a ball where you want it to go. I'm sure that even in your worst moments you don't want to hurt the people you're playing with.

I always remind people to start with the obvious. You're out in the fresh air, playing golf. How bad can it really be? It's just you and a little ball. Do you really want to admit that the ball is stronger than you are? Then use your pride to go in the other direction, away from making a jackass out of yourself.

I remember an incident that happened right here in my hometown at Miami Country Club. A local doctor and his son-in-law were playing golf on a nice afternoon. The son-in-law was struggling and after yet another bad shot he slammed his club to the ground. Not realizing that he had broken the club in two, he reared back to throw it. But because there was no head left on the shaft, his timing was off. The sharp edges of the broken shaft caught him in the arm and ripped a gash that quickly drew blood.

The doctor tossed him a towel and told him to wrap the wound. Then he proceeded to play his next shot.

The shaken son-in-law looked up and said. "I think we need to get to the hospital. This is bad."

His father-in-law shook his head in disgust. "I guess you'll have to find a good doctor on duty," he said. "I've got a round of golf to play." The son-in-law went to the hospital alone, got 22 stitches, and never threw another club.

Here's a tip I give my junior golfers: Hold your anger until the end of the round. Then, if you still feel like you have to throw something, go find an empty room and let it all out. Odds are, if you hold your temper until the end of the round, you'll be more interested in doing something constructive. Temper tantrums aren't much fun when you're by yourself.

Finishing the Round

I don't care how good you are for the first 13 or 14 holes, the real judge of a round comes at the end. If you can finish well, you'll find yourself winning more matches and setting more personal bests. And that's why we all tee it up in the first place. Pressure is something you face every day in your business and with your family. You handle it well there. Why should your golf game be any different?

I like to look at a round of golf as a series of three-hole stretches. That keeps it from being too big. I know that I can gear myself up and get out there and perform for three or four holes. You've got to be able to break things down on those finishing holes so that your mind doesn't wander off to how many strokes over or under your target score you are. It doesn't really matter anyway. All you can do is play those finishing holes as well as you can.

That's where hitting your second shot first comes in. If you want to reach your peak, you've got to defeat the pressure. Otherwise, your muscles get tight and you start thinking mechanically. Then you're dead. On the last few holes, you need to really focus on staying relaxed and swinging the golf club. Don't think about the result of the shot. You'll deal with that soon enough. The key is to stay positive and stay loose. Visualize great shots you've hit before. Then take yourself out of the pressure situation by enjoying your surroundings and savoring the moment.

You can find examples of people dealing with pressure all around you. I've been a lifelong fan of Oklahoma Sooner football. Now, there's no lonelier man in the world than a placekicker, in a tight game, as the clock winds down. Some years ago Oklahoma played a game against Ohio State in Columbus, not a real friendly place for visiting teams. Woody Hayes was still coaching the Buckeyes. Hayes was as much a gamesman as any golfer, and when this game came down to a field goal attempt by the Sooners, he went to work.

Oklahoma's kicker was a kid named Uwe VonSchamman. He trotted out onto the field, and Woody Hayes called a timeout. VonSchamman knew that the wily coach was trying to "ice" him – or make him think about the pressure. A lot of kickers would have stood there, rehearsing their kick over and over. But the bottom line is that VonSchamman already knew his pre-kick routine. The last thing you want to do is extend that routine. It's designed to last only so long. So while the student section chanted "block that kick, block that kick," and the Ohio State band played its loudest fight song, what did the Oklahoma kicker do? He walked over to the side of the field and started directing the band, waving his arms around like a maestro. What he did, you see, was "stop and smell the flowers." Rather than adding pressure by letting the distraction knock him out of his routine, he took his mind off of the situation. When the teams came back to the field, he stepped behind the ball, went through his normal routine, and drilled a 47-yard field goal through the uprights to win. He went on to a successful career with the Miami Dolphins. How does this story relate to your golf came? You figure that one out. And next time you find yourself in a pressure situation, remember that giving your mind a break can be the best way to prepare it for the task at hand. Don't extend your routine. Just be ready when the shot comes, and then do what you already know how to do. The results will take care of themselves.

CHAPTER 7

Driving the Ball

To me, playing golf is like painting. It takes all kinds of brush strokes to complete a picture – long, colorful ones and short ones placed just right. It's the same way on the golf course. That's what makes driving the ball so important. When you stand on the tee box and look down that fairway, you're staring at a blank canvas. The drive is going to be the first – and boldest – stroke you're going to paint on the hole. After that, you're filling everything in.

There's nothing that feels better than hitting a drive right in the sweetspot. When you're driving the ball well, you swing with confidence and you leave yourself high-percentage approach shots onto the greens. With all the rewards that come from a good drive, it surprises me that the driver is the club the amateur golfer fears the most. You don't have to hit it as far as Tiger Woods to be good with the driver. It is the biggest weapon in your bag, and to play your best golf you have to be able to use it. The secret is: It's simple.

On the Box

Watch the players who drive the ball best. They begin executing the shot before they even stick a tee in the ground. The entire hole is laid out before you – see what I mean by a blank canvas? You've got to decide what type of stroke will lay the groundwork for everything that's going to come next. Here are a couple of things to consider on the tee box.

Unless you're a better golfer than I've run across in the 50 years I've been teaching, you should always play away from the trouble. What you want to do is give yourself as much of a safety margin as you can. If there's water on the right, tee the ball up on the right side of the tee box. That sets you up to play to the left side. If your ball goes straight, you're in perfect shape. If it goes left, you're playing into open territory. If you hit it right, you've got a good chance of staying in the fairway and still having a good shot to the green.

I want you to think big on your tee shots. So you need a big target. Find a nice puffy cloud that's on your flight line. Then hit the ball right into that cloud. You'll get a good trajectory because your mind will be focused on getting the ball up. And you'll swing more freely because you've eliminated the target pressure that comes from trying to hit a certain spot on the fairway. God loves a thinking person. Pick a target somewhere between you and God.

It's All a Setup

The key to a good golf swing – and this is especially true with the driver – is a good setup. You'll never be consistent without mastering the fundamentals of the setup, and when your driver goes haywire, come back to them. That's a correction you can make in the middle of the round.

All good drivers are balanced over the ball. If you don't have balance to begin with, you won't find it once the swing begins. So start by getting your weight on the balls of your feet. Stand tall, with your left side higher than the right. I like to tell my students that you need to copy an airplane coming in for a landing. That way, you'll be sure to sweep through the hitting area. Hold your head high. The normal head weighs about 14 pounds. When you drop it down so that your chin is close to your chest, it becomes an obstacle and a burden for the swing to support. Keep your chin up.

Almost everybody I've ever taught is looking for more power off the tee. If you want more power, you're going to have to learn to set up behind the ball. Not only will staying well behind the ball allow your hands and arms to make a better release, it will give you a better visual line for more accuracy. The best power driver I've ever seen was the baseball great Mickey Mantle. His strength was in staying behind the ball, and he could hit it a mile. If your head and body get in front of the ball on the downswing, you'll have a hard time finding the sweetspot – or the fairway.

Karate black belts are some of the most powerful athletes in the world. They don't generate their force with raw strength. They learn how to get the most out of controlled motions. Watch a karate expert prepare to execute a move. You'll see that it all starts with the way he sets his body. The discipline of a proper setup is just as crucial in driving the ball. It makes you ready for action.

Tempo and Timing

If you've mastered a good setup, the swing will flow more naturally, but you'll still need good tempo and timing to drive the ball as long and straight as you can. There are good slow swings and good fast swings. The secret of all good swings, though, is rhythm. Start your swing by making sure that the club, hands, arms, and left knee all move away from the ball together. Now nothing has to "catch up" during the swing.

Most people tend to overturn in a search for more power. Overturning will rob you of everything you're trying to gain with the driver. The truth is, it's your hands and fingers that generate clubhead speed. You can't belly-whip the ball. As you take the club away, keep it low to the ground. Then let the wrists cock. You'll know when you've reached a comfortable position for the top of your swing, and your turn will come naturally.

From the top of your swing, think about making a nice, smooth transition. Too many players jerk their right shoulder and try to hit the ball with their arms, from the top. You know the result. You'll hit it fat or top it or hit big hooks and slices. Instead, think about making a throw to second base. At the top of the swing, you should be positioned to throw out a runner trying to steal. Don't think about third base or first base. Now just let it go.

The Secret's All Around You

The secret to good driving is all around you. Watch how someone sweeps with a broom. Do you see them making a long, jerky motion? No. It's a simple motion with the hands controlling and the body helping out. That's what a good golf swing is. Maybe the best thing you can do is take a kid to the playground and go to the swing set. As you push someone on a swing set, what to do you do? You balance yourself and make a nice, rhythmic push, staying back and releasing with your hands and arms. The result is a smooth, but powerful stroke. Now try to recreate that feeling on the tee box.Hitting long, straight drives is one of the greatest pleasures in golf. And like everything else, the keys to power and accuracy are simple. Setup, balance, and tempo. If you're looking for something more than that, you're playing the wrong game.

CHAPTER 8

Get Out of Jail

Golf is a lot easier when you play from the fairway. But no matter how good a player you are, that's not where you're always going to be. The most accurate players on the PGA Tour only hit the fairway seven out of ten times. What does that tell you? Knowing how to get out of jail is a key to scoring well.

Most people try to overpower the ball when they get into the long stuff. That's a big mistake. The most important part of hitting good escape shots is to strike the ball cleanly. What you really want to do is make the most simple swing you can – that's the swing that will help you get the clubface on the ball squarely for the best result. If you can make solid contact you shouldn't have too much trouble making good scores even when your driver is a little wayward.

Know Your Range

Most people would rate Seve Ballesteros as the best trouble player of all time. Even when he was winning major championships, he would be spraying drives all over the place. But the secret to Seve's ability to play out of trouble is that he knows when not to be a hero. Seve has incredible touch and feel around the greens. He knew that if he could just move the ball close to the green, he would have a good chance of getting up and down. There's another reason for you to get out there and work on your short game. It makes all the other parts of your game look better!

When Seve finds trouble, he always designs a safe escape route. You need to do the same thing. Assess your position and establish your goals. If the rough is light, you may be able to go for the green with any club up to a three-wood. But if the rough is heavy and the green is surrounded by sand or other hazards, you should plan on laying up unless you're in short-iron range. No matter what you're trying to do from the weeds, avoid long irons – there's not enough loft to get the ball airborne and the hosel almost always gets tangled up in the grass, closing the clubface even more. Then you have got real trouble, because you'll be playing from the rough again. Job one is to get back onto the golf course.

Most shots from the rough are going to come out low and without a lot of backspin. You should look for a path to run the ball whenever possible. Pay close attention to the position of the pin and the placement of trouble spots around the green. If a well-struck shot can get you to the green and leave you with a reasonable putt, go for it. If not, pick an open area that will give you the best chance at getting up and down. You'll quickly become the Seve of your regular foursome. It will drive your opponents nuts.

Hold On and Swing

The swing you need to make to escape the rough is not too different from the one you'd make from the fairway, but you do need to make a few adjustments. Start with your grip. The grass is going to try to turn the clubface in your hands. If it does, you lose any hope of keeping the ball straight. So you need to get a good firm grip with your left hand. This will help you maintain a square clubface throughout the swing and will also help you keep your hands quiet as you swing through the ball – both keys to hitting low, accurate shots from the rough.

Now that you're holding on, you can set up to make clean contact. I prepare for this shot just like I do for a fairway bunker shot. Take a slightly wider stance – about the width of your shoulders – to decrease body movement during the swing. Play the ball in the middle of your stance and put your weight mostly on the left side. This encourages you to hit down on the ball with the hands leading. You have to make good, clean contact with the ball first when playing from the rough. Position your head slightly behind the ball. Even though most of your weight is on the left side, you need to keep your upper body behind the ball or you'll block your release and decrease your chances of a good shot.

The swing itself is mostly arms. You want to make a three-quarters backswing. Think of your hands going back to shoulder-high. Be sure to take the club straight back away from the ball, again setting up a strong descending blow as you swing through. Keep your right elbow in close to your body. This helps to keep the swing short and keeps you from lifting your body during the backswing – a prime cause of mis-hits.

Think tempo for this swing. It's just an easy "one-two" time, back and through. You'll get much more power by hitting the ball in the center of the clubface than you will by muscling the clubhead through the grass.

Stay behind the ball as you swing through, and think about leading with your hands. If you keep your wrists firm, you'll finish in a nice, low position. And now you'll be back on the course, ready to try to save par.

Get Creative

When the rough isn't too deep, you may have the opportunity to work the ball from right to left or left to right. You can do this with the same setup adjustments and swing that we've already discussed. To put curve on the ball, just change your alignment while keeping the clubface aimed square to the target.

If you need a left-to-right shot, aim your body left of the target and swing the club along the body's line to create the slice spin. Likewise, for a right-to-left shot, aim to the right to put hook spin on the ball.

You'll also find yourself in need of a high shot from the rough from time to time. You should only try to go over trees in your path if you have a nice lie that will let you get the clubhead underneath the ball. If that's the case, move the ball up toward your left heel in the stance, set your head a little farther behind the ball, and swing away. If the shot is outside of nine iron or wedge distance, take an extra club, aim slightly left, and open the face a bit to add loft. I've seen players hit pop-up shots 160-yards by opening the face of a six iron, although I'd recommend you practice with an eight iron first to get the feel.

Drive Under Trouble

Now here's a great shot that almost anyone can hit. If you have a good lie in shallow rough or even on the side of the fairway and you need to play a low shot under tree limbs, take a driver. That's right, a driver. It's the easiest club in the bag to hit, because it has the biggest face. The length of the club will help you put a smooth swing on it, and the overspin guarantees you'll get a lot of run on the ball.

This shot is great for distances outside of about 160 or 170 yards,

CHAPTER 9

Etiquette: The Golfer's Code of Respect

Make no mistake, the game of golf is its own society, and like every society, there are laws and ethics. We'll get to the laws in just a bit, but first let's spend a little time on etiquette, or the way you treat your fellow golfers during a round. Our world has become less civil. We hear about shootings on freeways and we see people treated with a general lack of respect all around us. I like to believe that golf is above that. Our game is for gentlemen and ladies. Now you may think that sounds old-fashioned, but I'll tell you that old-fashioned isn't so bad when it comes to treating each other right. Golf is a tie that binds us together, and if we want to keep it that way, etiquette is the best place to start. If you follow the basic guidelines of golf etiquette, you will become a positive role model every time you tee it up, and the entire society of golf will be better for it.

Etiquette and the Golden Rule

I've worked with thousands of junior golfers during my life. I've seen some of them go on to great college and professional careers in the game. Most of them, however, go into more traditional careers and play golf for fun. But this much is certain: Every young player I work with comes out of our sessions knowing the etiquette of golf. I've always believed in the Golden Rule – do unto others as you would have them do unto you. That's etiquette in a nutshell.

You wouldn't want to eat dinner with someone who chewed with his mouth open or clanged silverware loudly on the dishes throughout the meal. And you wouldn't want to play golf with someone who shows no consideration for you and your game. Golf is going to give you chances to get to know people who can change your life. Don't mess it up by being sloppy on the course and making the day a frustrating experience.

Etiquette begins on the first tee. Greet all the players in your group with a firm handshake and wish them luck. Make sure you know everybody's name. You're getting ready to spend four hours of your life with these folks. Why would you want to treat them like strangers? If I'm playing with new people, I make a note on the scorecard so I can remember their names. The winners in business never forget names. Neither do the winners in golf.

Almost everybody knows to be quiet when another player is swinging. But you should take it one step further than that and give each player a chance to prepare for each shot in silence. I'd rather have you talking during my backswing than yammering on while I'm going through my pre-shot routine. That's the source of your concentration.

Stand clear of a player's line during his shot. Don't forget that the line runs not only from the ball to the hole but back from the ball and well past the hole as well. Position yourself out of the player's view by standing still, well off to the side.

Keep your hands out of your pockets while the other players in your group are playing their shots. It's easy to get "rabbit ears" on the golf course, where you hear almost everything. Sam Snead's putting difficulties are legendary. To perform on the greens, he needed all the concentration he could muster. During one tournament, a lady following Snead's group was carrying coins in her pocket. As she stood off to the side of the green, she would absentmindedly jingle the coins with her hand. She never meant to distract anyone, but the constant rattle at every green drove Snead crazy. Finally, Snead found a solution. After holing out, he went and found the woman in the gallery.

"Ma'am," he said, fishing a dollar bill out of his own pocket, "do you have change for a dollar?"

The key to practicing good etiquette is just to stay aware. Know where your shadow falls and try to keep it out of your fellow players' line of sight. If you realize that you don't have time to move before they play, stay still. It's not too much trouble to play through a shadow, but one that's moving can be a real annoyance.

Don't step in a player's line when you're on the green. You may not even leave a mark on the green, but you'll surely make an impression in the minds of the other golfers in your group. Failing to pay attention to the games of your partners is just as much a breach of etiquette as purposely interfering.

Hurry Up and Miss It

The most common etiquette violation in golf is slow play. You don't play better golf by taking longer to do it, and you don't have to rush to play at a good pace. Playing at a good pace is a courtesy that extends to the groups in front of you and behind you – and to everybody on the golf course during your round.

Too many people confuse bad play with slow play. I've known plenty of bad golfers who never held up play on a golf course. They're more conscious of playing slowly than just about anyone else. The worst slow-play culprits are often the better players. They're the ones who fidget and fuss the most. The PGA Tour is a swamp of slow play. Now, I admire Jack Nicklaus so much for everything he's accomplished in golf, but he is the worst slow player in the history of the game. He's not alone, of course. If golf courses were made of wet cement, Bernhard Langer, Nick Faldo and Tiger Woods would be statues by now.

I learned long ago that there's no excuse for a good player to be a slow player. The most telling lesson came from my good friend George Coleman. George was a native of my hometown who went on to great things in business and in golf. He won the Oklahoma State Amateur Championship in the 1930's. George traveled with Ky Lafoon on many road trips and met Bing Crosby, Bob Hope – and a young Texan named Ben Hogan. When wartime called all men to support the cause, George helped arrange for Ky and Ben to work at Spartan Aeronautics in Tulsa, where they could serve their country and continue to work on their golf games. These three remained friends throughout their lives.

Whether in the boardroom or on the golf course, George always made sure he treated people right. The most prestigious clubs in America sought him out as a member. He belonged to Augusta National and was president of Seminole Golf Club in Florida for many years. Their invitational tournament is named in his honor.

George Coleman detested slow play. He was a busy man, and he saw time wasted as time lost. The last thing he wanted to do was stand around waiting for someone to get ready to play. When it came George's turn to play, he already had his glove on, knew his distance and had his club selected. "If you're gonna miss it," he said to me more than once, "just hurry up and miss it. I don't have all day."

I've never forgotten that.

Be Ready

You hear so much these days about playing "ready golf," where the person ready to hit goes ahead and plays, regardless of the honor or the position of his ball. I'll tell you now that I'm not a big fan of that kind of ready golf. Using the honor on the tee box and the traditional order of play through the green is a great part of the game. But that doesn't mean you can't play quickly. The key is to be ready when it's your turn.

Although there are a thousand instructors out there who might tell you otherwise, there's not much science to hitting a golf ball. Figure your yardage, select your club, and play the shot. Your routine should be well under way while the other members of your group are playing their shots. Don't wait until your turn rolls around to start pulling your glove out of your pocket and start pacing yardages.

Being ready means being ready to move to the next hole as well. When you get to the green, do everyone on the course a favor and leave your cart or bag between the green and the next tee. Making the next group wait while you go all the way back across the green after holing out is a sure way to make enemies.

Finally, pick the darn ball up when you're out of the hole (except in tournament play, of course). Some courses have a "double-par" rule. That means when you get to eight shots on a par-4 and still haven't holed out, pick it up. I say that should be the absolute latest you pick up the ball. Everybody struggles on a hole every now and then. If you have a handicap, you have certain maximum scores you can take. When you reach them, put the ball in your pocket and concentrate on doing better on the next hole.

How to Play Through

No matter how quickly you play, there will always be groups who play even faster. I have a neighbor and business partner who is a member of the beautiful Bighorn Country Club in Palm Desert, California. It was there that I saw the fastest group of golfers I've ever seen. The owner of the Bighorn development loves golf, but even more than that he loves high-speed golf. I've only seen him once, and that was all it took for me to know I'd never see a faster player.

We were on the 10th hole, and our forecaddie waved me over to the side of the fairway.

"That's the owner and his group back on the tee," the caddie said. "You might as well let them play through."

We waved them through and waited for them to motor down the fairway to play their approach shots. Before we even knew it, they had jumped out of their carts, hit the balls, and were nothing but four backs disappearing down the fairway in souped-up golf carts.

"How do they stand?" our caddie asked the owner's forecaddie as we stood off to the side.

"Fifty-five minutes to here. They're taking it easy today."

Now I don't believe that golf should be a race. My point is only that there will be times when you just have to let another group play through, so you might as well know how to do it properly. Otherwise, you'll botch up the flow of the entire golf course. At Bighorn it was easy – there was no one else around. That won't be the case most of the time.

Playing through or having another group play through is a last resort. Don't do it until you've made every effort to pick up your pace. If you're keeping pace with the group in front you, don't worry about being pushed from behind – there's nowhere you can go. But if you do have to let someone through, it's a lot easier if you know what you're doing.

The best place to let a group through is on the green. Mark your balls, step aside, and wave the group through. Then, while they are making their way to the green, go ahead and putt out. You can then move to the next tee box, where you can wait for the group to hole their putts and let them go ahead off the next tee. That way, you haven't held up play. You've just reordered the foursomes. That's the idea. Don't let a group play through just because you're looking for a lost ball. If you've looked until play has backed up behind you, you've spent too much time looking already. Let it go. Any time you let a group play through in the middle of a hole, you're disrupting traffic.

And that's poor etiquette.

Should you find yourself stuck behind a slow group, resist the temptation to get angry. They may not know they are holding you up. You should never, ever hit into the group in front of you. That only raises tensions and creates ugly situations. Instead, wait for an opportunity when you can speak with the group and ask if you can play through at the next tee or on the next green. They'll almost always say yes if you approach the situation with kindness. If they are out of position and fail to let you through, consult a course ranger or the head professional. Taking matters into your own hands can only lead to trouble.

A Few Words on Cell Phones

As the world changes, so does the game of golf. Wireless communication has changed the way that business operates, and it's changed the way we live. One of the products of all this change is that more and more people now bring cellular phones with them onto the golf course.

I've heard all kinds of opinions about cell phones on the course. The fact of the matter is that they're here to stay, so we have to integrate their use into the etiquette of the game. I think it's wonderful that people who might not otherwise be able to get out and spend an afternoon on the golf course can now do it because of this technology. I'll make the same argument for the use of golf carts. Yes, I miss the days of everybody walking, but I'm happy that golf carts let people keep on playing golf well into the later years of their lives.

There's no reason that cell phones should bother anyone on a golf course, if the owners of these phones would follow a few simple rules. I don't know if anyone else has done it or not, but here's my proposal for cell phone etiquette on the golf course.

1. Don't receive incoming calls. If you're savvy enough to own a cell phone, you should know how to use voice mail and caller ID to get an idea of who is trying to reach you without annoying your fellow players with a ringing telephone.

2. Don't hold up play. If the cell phone is causing you to be unprepared to play your shot when it's your turn, then you are displaying poor etiquette. Get out of the golf cart and walk to your ball, using that time to make your phone call. Make the person on the other end of the phone wait while you play your shot. On the golf course, respect for your fellow players is more important than the convenience of the person on the other end of the line.

3. Step away from your group. The members of your group didn't ask you to bring the phone with you. If you're aware of how you use it, it shouldn't bother them. But when you hold a conversation right in the middle of your foursome, you make them feel like they have to be quiet in order not to disturb you. Step away so they can carry on as they normally would on the course.

I don't see any excuse for poor etiquette. Learn the basics of moving around the course quickly and pleasantly. Then make sure that you're always asking yourself how your actions are affecting those around you. If you do that, people should always enjoy playing golf with you.

CHAPTER 10

The Rules of Golf

If you are to be a contributing member of our society, you need to know laws of the land and make every effort to uphold them. I don't think it's asking too much that you familiarize yourself with the Rules of Golf. The laws of our states and countries give us a sense of order about how we earn our livings and conduct our personal lives. You may not believe a certain law is right, but that doesn't mean you're free to break it. Golf is the same way, except that the Rules of Golf may be even more complex than the laws of most countries, and more painful.

The Rules of Golf define the way we play the game. They serve as an objective judge. What if we all played by our own rules? Fair competition and handicapping would be impossible. This is why I implore you – as I do all my students – to play golf by the rules. That means accepting a bad lie, even if your ball comes to rest in a divot. It means swallowing your pride and returning to the tee if you lose your drive, incurring the severe stroke-and-distance penalty rather than just dropping a ball in the approximate area of your original ball. No matter how unfair the rules may seem to you during a friendly round, remember that far greater golfers have bowed to them when far more was at stake.

Golf is the only game where the player is responsible for enforcing the rules. That means that you have a direct responsibility to the game. There are many examples you can use to console yourself when you end up on the short side of the rules. And these often heartbreaking moments have become defining moments in golf. Adhering to the rules shows integrity and respect – the very foundations of golf.

Think of Bob Dickson. Dickson was one of the top amateurs of his time. In the second round of the 1965 U.S. Amateur, which was then conducted at stroke play, he made a horrible discovery. He was carrying a 15th club. Dickson knew there was only one thing he could do, and that was to penalize himself. He called the violation and took two-stroke penalties on the first and second holes. Unfortunately, someone had placed the extra club in his bag by mistake. Even more unfortunately, Dickson had failed to count his clubs before teeing off. To cap it all off, Dickson finished second by a single shot in the tournament. He later went on to win both the U.S. Amateur and British Amateur championships. His rules violation became a measure of his ability to accept the reality of golf and ended up helping his development as a player.

The Unkindest Ruling of All

No one can argue that the Rules of Golf can be cold and ruthless – even for those who must make the final interpretations. One of my favorite golf partners when I was younger was John Winters. John and I played golf at Southern Hills in Tulsa every Thursday and Sunday. I remain good friends with John's son Otis to this day. John Winters loved golf and went on to become a president of the USGA and a member of Augusta National. At the 1967 Masters, John found himself personally involved in the heartbreaking story of Roberto De Vicenzo.

De Vicenzo was a popular player on the tour, and things could hardly have gone better for him during the final round. It was his birthday. He holed his approach shot for eagle at the first hole, shot 31 on the front, and then stormed through the back nine, surging to eight under par on the day with a birdie on the 17th hole. Just when it looked like he would clinch his first major tournament victory, De Vicenzo bogeyed the final hole for 65 and fell into a tie with Bob Goalby. The playoff would take place the following day.

De Vicenzo and his fellow competitor Tommy Aaron proceeded to the scorer's tent to review their scores and sign their cards to make the round official. Aaron correctly showed a total of 65 on De Vicenzo's card, but somehow he had mis-marked the 17th hole, recording a four instead of the three De Vicenzo actually made. De Vicenzo, caught up in the excitement, failed to notice the error and signed the scorecard. When the officials added up the scores, the total read 66 because of the mis-marked hole, not 65 as Aaron had noted.

Millions of people had witnessed De Vicenzo's round on TV, and the rules committee frankly didn't want to see the Masters decided on such a technicality. After much discussion, my friend John Winters, along with Augusta National rules committee members Ike Grainger and Hord Hardin, took the issue all the way to Bobby Jones, who was by then bedridden with disease.

Bobby Jones listened as the rules officials described the situation, and he asked that the specific rule be read to him aloud.

"If the competitor returns a score for any hole lower than actually played, he shall be disqualified. A score higher than actually played must stand as returned."

Jones, a quintessential sportsman who had called several violations on himself during his glorious playing career, then made what would be his final statement on the honor of the game of golf. "Well," he said. "There is no other choice. That must be the decision."

Never once in all the years since then has De Vicenzo cried foul. He has simply cried for what might have been. And his grace in handling such a painful ruling has earned him a place as one of the great sportsmen of his time.

Knowledge is Power

I will give you this piece of advice: Go out and buy a Rules Book. Then study it, particularly if you ever plan to play in competitions. The USGA conducts workshops all around the country every year. Attend one. By knowing the rules, you will know the game as all the greats have played it and you become a custodian of the most honorable sport on earth.

I am disturbed by the lack of rules awareness that we see today on the PGA Tour. Davis Love III ended up being disqualified at the 1997 Player's Championship after accidentally hitting his ball while taking a practice stroke with his putter. Love didn't know that the rules called for him to replace his ball to its original position at a penalty of one stroke. Instead, he took a one-stroke penalty and played it from its new position. Failure to replace the ball carries a separate penalty, and Davis ended up signing an incorrect scorecard and being disqualified because of his lack of knowledge. Amazingly, neither his caddie, nor his fellow competitor, nor the PGA Tour officials with the group noticed the secondary infraction.

I am reminded every day of the importance of knowing the rules. The reminder is a small sliver of wood that hangs on the wall of my house.

It was a gift to me from my friend Craig Stadler, and it came from the tree that starred in one of golf's most bizarre rulings ever.

Craig was in the thick of contention on Saturday afternoon at the 1987 Andy Williams Classic, played at Torrey Pines Golf Course in La Jolla, California. On the 14th hole he pushed his tee shot to the right of the fairway, and the ball came to rest under a tree. Craig has always been an imaginative player, and rather than take an unplayable lie penalty he decided to play the shot from a kneeling position. Now, any of you who have traveled to San Diego in the winter know that you can get showers from time to time. The ground was damp, and Craig neatly folded a towel, knelt on it, and played a great shot back to the fairway. He finished the round, signed his scorecard, and came to the golf course on Sunday ready to play for the title.

Craig did play on Sunday, eventually finishing second in the tournament. Unfortunately for him, however, NBC had been replaying the towel shot from the day before throughout the final round telecast. A viewer who saw the highlights of Saturday's round, on TV, called the PGA Tour rules official at the scene and explained that according to the Rules of Golf, the towel represented "building a stance" through artificial means; a clear violation of rule 13-3. Craig may only have tried to keep his pants dry, but the rules are the rules. The tour assessed him a penalty, thereby changing his score for that hole. Since Craig had already signed his scorecard with an incorrect lower score, he was disqualified from the tournament. His lack of knowledge of the rules had cost him $37,000.

Later, Craig confessed that he had not sat down and read the Rules of Golf in some time. He vowed to do it and did, and he has stayed free of controversy and had a very successful career since then – even winning in San Diego a few years ago on that same Torrey Pines course. When the operators of Torrey Pines decided a couple of years ago to remove the tree from the 14th hole, they called Craig to fire up the chainsaw and do the honors, which he was happy to do.

Shortly after that, I got my piece of the tree.

Local Rules

As you study to become a rules expert, don't forget to note how local rules affect play at any given course or in any given tournament.

Local rules are established by club or tournament officials and are designed to govern situations specific to the course or event. You will find local rules on the scorecard of a golf course or on the tournament handout sheet in a competition.

Some of these local rules can have a dramatic effect on play. On the PGA Tour, players can receive "line-of-sight" relief from scoreboards and grandstands. What had been an impossible shot can become an easy pitch, as Ernie Els found out when he drove the ball far left of the 17th fairway at Oakmont in the final round of the 1994 U.S. Open. Because the grandstands are temporary immovable obstructions, he received line-of-sight relief and ended up with an easy shot to the green.

The "one-ball rule" that requires a player to use only one type of ball throughout an entire competitive round is actually a local rule implemented on a tournament-by-tournament basis. So is the "lift, clean, and place" rule hated by the USGA but often used on the PGA Tour.

Local rules often present a lighter side of golf. I remember playing the old Sawgrass Country Club a few years ago with my son, who was just a young boy at the time. As young Marshall headed up the 12th fairway to play his second shot, he stopped in his tracks. There, just feet away from his ball, a large alligator was sunning himself. Luckily, local rules provided relief by letting Marshall drop another ball without having to retrieve his original one. Of course, I might have insisted that he violate the rules and do that anyway, but you get the point.

Calling a Violation

There's nothing that will make you more uncomfortable on the golf course than having to call a rules violation on another player. The effects of making the call can linger forever. During the Skins Game a few years ago, Tom Watson accused Gary Player of failing to call a penalty on himself, saying that Player's ball moved while Player was removing a leaf. Those two will still hardly speak to each other. At the 1995 World Series of Golf, Greg Norman accused fellow competitor Mark McCumber of removing spike marks from the line of his putts. McCumber claimed he was removing bugs. Though the PGA Tour did not assess a penalty on McCumber, his reputation was sullied, and he has not been a regular on the tour since. These are very high profile examples, but you can probably think of similar examples that happened much closer to home. Any instance that calls a person's honor into question is a serious one.

The most important rule you can follow is to remember that you don't enforce the rules on another player. Instead, you call a suspected violation to his attention. Don't wait until after the round and then bring it up with a tournament official. If you feel that he has committed an infraction, you should be able to address it with the player directly. After all, it is up to him to enforce the rule on himself. I always make that call by asking a question rather than making an accusation.

"Did you see that ball move?" I might ask.

If he says no, I have two options: Take him at his word or, if I feel strongly enough, refuse to sign his scorecard at the end of the round. If we're just out for an informal round, I probably won't make a big deal about it, though I'd hesitate to play with that person again. In tournament play or in a money match, I might challenge his answer if I don't believe it.

You should also keep in mind that in golf, most rules infractions are involuntary and are often the result of a lack of rules knowledge. If I see a player making an improper drop – after hitting a ball into a lateral water hazard, for instance – or taking relief when not entitled to it, I'll suggest what I think is the correct procedure. If there is disagreement, I urge the player to play two balls – one from the position he believes to be correct and one from the position I feel is right. Then we can consult the head professional or a tournament official later and get a ruling. Now we haven't held up play, and hopefully we haven't started an argument.

Occasionally you will end up in a match with someone who is a real rules stickler. That is within his right, but he should not be surprised if you turn the tables. My co-author Tom Ferrell tells a story of being involved in a match during the club championship at his home club in Georgia when he was younger. Teeing off on the 11th hole, a par-4 with water running down both sides of the fairway, Tom played a long iron to the middle of the fairway.

"Nice shot," his opponent said. "Too bad you are going to have to hit it over." He went on to point out that Tom had inadvertently teed his ball a few inches in front of the tee markers.

There was no question that Tom had teed off in front of the markers. In match play there is no penalty for this offense, but you must replay the ball from within the teeing ground. Tom's replay found the water. He then hit his approach shot over the green, nearly out of bounds, while his opponent knocked a wedge close to the pin. Tom then chipped in for par. His opponent left his birdie putt a few inches short of the hole. In disgust, he quickly stepped to the ball and slapped it over the back of the green, out of bounds.

Tom claimed the hole. His opponent claimed the putt was short enough to be considered "good," but Tom pointed out that he had not conceded the putt, due mainly to how quickly his opponent had stepped up and whacked the ball from the green. Facing an angry opponent, Tom questioned why three inches should matter more on a tee shot than on a short putt. The resulting discussion caused quite an uproar at the club, with some members feeling that Tom had taken advantage of his opponent while others believed that the opponent had set the tone for the strict rulings.

How would you feel in this situation?

The rules play a larger role in golf than in any other sport. I believe that part of considering yourself a golfer is to know and appreciate the rules and always strive to uphold them in every round you play. When you know and abide by the rules, you demonstrate a respect for the game. You will also stand to benefit from the rules by knowing all of your options when you are faced with difficult situations. More than anything else, however, a respect of the rules is a testament that you don't consider yourself larger than the game, and it is a link to everything that makes golf great.

CHAPTER 11

Competition

People play golf for many reasons. But I've never bought into the idea of playing golf purely for relaxation. Deep down inside, the game of golf is a competitive spirit. No other sport offers as many competitive possibilities, whether we're talking about friendly wagers with your buddies or national championships. Vince Lombardi was wrong when he said that winning was the "only thing." It's the competition itself that makes you feel alive. Golf is not about proving anything to anyone else. It's about proving something to yourself. That's why competition is so important.

When you reach down inside and find that there is something there, you know that your hard work has paid off. On those occasions when you lose, you learn even more about yourself and your game. In order to develop a competitive game, you need disicpline, patience, faith, and a good work ethic. Is it any surprise that a person who displays these traits on the golf course often carries that success into his or her other endeavors as well?

So many golfers ask me how they'll know when they're ready for competition. I believe that you're ready as soon as you start thinking about it. Competition gives you so many opportunities to learn and achieve and to meet other people who love golf and love the thrill of testing their games against their nerves. Go for it.

Over-Practicing

If there's one mistake I see in golfers who are new to competition or who compete too infrequently, it's that they over-practice. Rather than staying in their normal rhythm, they start "preparing" weeks in advance. Competition is an extension of your game, not something totally different. If you tend to play rather than practice heavily, why on earth would you suddenly start going to the driving range two weeks before a tournament? That's going to get you out of your rhythm.

Dr. Gil Morgan is one of the finest golfers the state of Oklahoma has ever produced. I can't even remember a time that I've seen him on the practice tee if it wasn't just to loosen up before a round. Gil is a player, not a practicer. The most famous non-practicer on the PGA Tour is Bruce Lietzke. Bruce's caddie once claimed to have put a banana under the headcover of Bruce's driver at the end of tournament. Bruce then took one of his frequent long breaks from the tour. Six weeks later, at the end of the break, the caddie pulled the headcover off of the driver as they were about to warm up for the first round. The banana was still there, although it was in much worse shape after the layoff than Bruce's swing.

I've only known a handful of players who had the talent to base their games on mechanics. Ben Hogan was one of them. Tom Kite is another. Tom uses practice as a meditation, a way to clear his mind. He relies on confidence in his mechanics, and he needs a lot of practice time as a result. But Tom has a tremendous understanding of the golf swing, which is hard to develop if you haven't spent an entire lifetime at it. Nick Faldo has tried for years to base his game on mechanics, but I think it's hurt him as much as it's helped him. You have to be able to win even when your swing is a little off.

The message here is there is no right or wrong way for you to get ready for competition. But there is a right way and wrong way for you to prepare. Your challenge is to recognize what works for you and have the faith to stick with it. If you're playing well, you're preparing well. If not, try a different way of getting ready.

One of the easiest ways to tell if you're preparing properly is to look at the way you play the first few holes of your competitive rounds. Do you tend to get uptight on the first tee and make mistakes on the early holes? If you do, it's probably because you have been practicing too much or warming up too much before the round. After a few holes you forget about all the mechanical thoughts you tried to transfer from the range and you settle into a better frame of mind.

Most players would do much better to spend more practice time on their short games and on the putting green. Ball striking comes and goes, no matter how much you practice. When you focus on your short game, you learn to focus on saving strokes. That's what helps you lower your scores. Remember this: A good short game will bail you out of poorly struck shots much better than well-struck shots will make up for a poor short game.

Nerves

I'll just tell you right now that any player who tells you he's not nervous on the first tee of a big tournament or important round is lying. Maybe they don't mean to lie, but the simple truth is that you can't help getting nervous when you feel like you have something to prove. The pressure only increases if you play well for the first rounds of a tournament. And the sad fact is that sometimes you'll fail, no matter who you are. Who will ever forget that painful Sunday when Greg Norman, after three days of flawless golf, let the Masters championship he wants so badly slip away? There's no explanation for his final-round 78 other than nerves.

Tom Watson is one of the greatest winners of all time. In his prime, it was very rare for him to succumb to the pressure. It wasn't always that way. Watson first appeared on the professional scene at the 1974 U.S. Open at Winged Foot. Against a tough field and an even tougher golf course, the young pro held the lead after 54 holes and spent a fitful night tossing and turning and dreaming of being U.S. Open champion. The next day he shot 79. The following year he again held the lead after 54 holes, and again he folded. But later in that summer of 1975, Tom Watson won his first PGA Tour event, the Western Open. Then he won the BritishOpen. For the next decade he was the dominant player in golf.

What turned Tom Watson from a choker into a champion? He learned to stop complicating his game with visions of things he couldn't control – like victories. Instead, he learned to maintain his focus and concentrate simply on playing a good round of golf. He developed a strong sense of faith that if he just played well, the rest would take care of itself. And it did, time and time again.

The great winners rarely talk about winning. Instead, they talk about the thrill of being in the hunt. Winners thrive on the nerves that build as they close in on the final few holes of a tournament. The players who consistently fall a shot short fear those same nerves. Winners know that losing is just a step in their education. Losers fear that they will always be branded a loser if they fail.

You can't avoid getting nervous on the golf course. Who would want to? Getting nervous means you've played yourself into position to achieve a goal. Have you ever stood on the final tee knowing that you needed a par for a personal-best score? Tell me your hands weren't shaking. It's no coincidence that the first place you feel your nerves is in your hands. So that's where to start when finding the best way to deal with the pressure.

Your instinct when you get nervous is to tighten up. When you tighten up on the golf club, all sorts of bad things can happen. Try this: Next time you find yourself getting nervous, whether you're on the first tee of a big match or coming down the stretch with a chance to set a personal best or win a tournament, shake out your hands. Go on and shake them out like a swimmer getting ready for the start of a race. Flick your fingers in a 1-2-3-4 rhythm. Now take three deep breaths and go through your regular pre-shot routine. Don't worry about the result. You've already achieved something simply by playing into a position to get nervous. There is no failure from here, only experience.

Patience

Tournament golf is a lot like prize fighting. The last one left standing is often the one who wins. This means you have to be patient and prevent isolated mistakes from piling up on each other. Most of all, you have to accept that you can't force something to happen. You have to be patient.

Curtis Strange has enjoyed a long career at the top levels of competitive golf. His greatest moment came when he won the 1989 U.S. Open at Oak Hill Country Club in Rochester, becoming the first person since Ben Hogan to successfully defend his title. In professional golf, the name of the game is usually birdies. But when you throw in a healthy dose of thick rough, fast greens, and U.S. Open pressure, everything changes. Although Curtis has at times shown a great deal of impatience with his golf game, this day was different. He started out three shots behind leader Tom Kite. But rather than coming out firing at the pins and trying to make up those shots quickly, he began with a methodical string of pars and just kept adding to it. All of a sudden Kite, who was struggling with the pressure of trying to win his first major championship, hit a wild tee shot and made triple-bogey. Now Curtis was tied for the lead. The pars just kept coming. Curtis missed a few birdie chances – some that he should have made. But he didn't allow himself to get aggressive. He just kept making pars. Soon he had played the front nine in all pars. Then he parred the first six holes on the back nine. Then, on the difficult 16th hole, a 25-foot birdie putt found the cup, almost by accident. That one birdie was all he needed. He finished his round with pars on seventeen and eighteen and raised his arms in victory.

Later, when someone asked him what his mindset was for that day, Curtis said, "I just tried to par the golf course to death."

What a great image of patience.

Learning a Golf Course

If you play a golf course enough times, you eventually learn how to score on it. You instinctively play away from trouble spots. You know where the scoring opportunities are and where disaster lurks. You know how the greens break and how the ball bounces. You know how the course plays when it's wet and how it plays when it's dry.

But when you're preparing for a competition, you'll be lucky to get one or two chances to see the golf course. That means you've got to learn it quickly. Your best shot at seeing how the course plays is your practice round.

Don't worry about your score during a practice round. You have to remember that the purpose of the round is education, not excellence. You'll use the information you gain during the practice round for your mental rehearsals and on-course decision making throughout the week. The idea is to learn as much about the course as possible.

Make notes on positioning off the tee box. What holes are good driver holes? Where should you hit an iron in order to lay up at your favorite distance for a good approach opportunity? You can't overpower a golf course, especially one that you haven't played many times. Start conservatively, and as you learn more about the course throughout the tournament, you can refine your game plan off the tee.

The real benefit of local knowledge of a golf course comes on and around the greens, and this is where you want to spend the most time during the practice round. Study the contours and shapes on the greens.

Where would the good pin positions be? Take a look at the penalties for missing the green short, to the sides, and long. Which areas give you the best chances to get up and down?

Does the course play long and soft or is it hard and fast? You have to know this so that you can practice the appropriate wedge shots and chips. On a wet course where there's not much run, you'll need to gear your short game to higher shots that fly most of the way to the pin. On a fast course, you may want to practice your Texas wedge shots and other bump and runs. Take as many notes as you can and review them later. If you take away the element of surprise from a golf course, you've taken away its greatest weapon. By playing a smart practice round, you'll be able to recognize a sucker pin before you've become the sucker. We've talked about it before: You can always recover from a bogey, but doubles hurt.

After your practice round, go directly to the short game area and, using your notes, work on the shots you'll need on the course. Imagine yourself playing specific shots to specific greens. Your mind doesn't know the difference between rehearsing on the practice green and rehearsing on the golf course. It just feels more prepared because of the rehearsal.

Play Your Game, Play to Win

Once the tournament begins, you need to trust in your game and yourself. The routines that work for you in friendly rounds with your buddies will work in tournament play, too. The key is to eliminate the dumb mistakes and let everything else take care of itself. Enjoy the fellowship of other serious players. Every time you play a competitve round, you're learning. You'll learn about the strengths and weaknesses of your own game, and you'll learn from the other players in the event. Over time, competition will improve your game more than a thousand hours on the practice tee ever could.

Add competition into every round you play. Don't create life or death situations, but always give yourself a prize to play for, whether it's a few bucks with your friends or something for yourself if you break a personal record on the course.

A golf writer I know was talking recently about an article he'd seen where a number of other golf writers were listing the greatest moments in golf. Most of them were picking Hogan's 1951 U.S. Open victory, Jack Nicklaus' 1986 Masters win and other high-profile victories by the game's top players. But my friend had a different take. He told me how he had gone out for nine holes at his local course one evening and was paired with two women. On the seventh tee, one of the women turned to him and said that it looked like she had a chance to break 60, on nine holes, for the first time.

"I've always said I'd treat myself to an expensive day at a spa if I did it," she said.

By the time they reached the ninth tee it had become quite dark. The woman squinted at her scorecard and said that she need a seven on the ninth, a tough par-4 with water down the right side, to achieve her goal. Her drive was a good one, down the fairway. Her second shot sounded good but flew into the darkness. After a few minutes of searching, she declared that it must have gone in the water.

"Well," my friend said, "that's tough to say. I think we could let you drop another one."

She shook her head. "No, I hit it at the water. I have to say that it went in."

She dropped her third and then duffed her fourth shot. With the tension rising and the darkness getting thicker, she duffed her fifth shot, too. The sixth shot was better but came to rest at the front of the green, some forty feet from the hole. Then, with my friend tending the flagstick, she rolled that forty-footer dead center into the cup for her seven.

I still get chills thinking about it," my friend confesses.

The woman leapt in the air, gave high-fives to her partner and my friend and let out a whoop that lit up the night.

"I've seen a lot of great moments in golf," my friend told me. "But never one any better than that."

That woman had won a major victory. She met adversity head on, emerged with her sense of honor intact, and pulled a little miracle up from deep inside.

Now if that's not winning, I just don't know what is.

CHAPTER 12

The 19th Hole: Reflections on the Game

For the people who really love it, golf isn't just a game. It's a way of living. In golf you find all sorts of lessons; on honor, patience and hard work, and - most of all - on friendship. The camaraderie of golfers is the single greatest element of the game. Take a look around you when you're in the 19th hole, after a round. It doesn't matter how well or how poorly you've played that day. In the lounge you're surrounded by friends and you're bound by the common experience. You may laugh at yourself and the show you put on during your round. Or you may sulk over the one or two missed shots that kept you from setting a personal best or winning a hard-fought bet. You may rejoice at how every bounce just seemed to go your way, as if an angel was on your side. But whatever it is that you're feeling, you won't be alone. In the 19th hole, you're surrounded by others who have been there before.

Not all the stories you'll hear at the 19th hole are true. But some of the whoppers people tell pack even bigger punches than a straight telling would. When it comes to sitting down with your fellow golfers, it's friendship and community that matters most.

I've been so fortunate in my life. I've had some success in business. I've been married for 35 years to a wonderful woman and raised kids who have grown into people I can admire and respect. They have become my favorite golf partners. I have also made more friends than I ever dreamed possible.

I've unlocked a lot of doors in my life, and more often than not, golf has been the key.

The game has helped my friends and me through some of the bad times as well. Just recently, my good friend Steve Owens lost his 25-year-old son. Most of us can only imagine how painful it would be to lose a child. I've spent a lot of time with Steve and his wife in the weeks and months since Blake's death, and I'm convinced that Blake's love of golf has given them something positive and pleasant to hold on to during the difficult times.

Blake Owens loved the game as much as anyone who ever played it. Even when he was most troubled, he found peace on the golf course. Steve remembers the days they spent together on the course at Shangri-La, our beautiful resort on the Grand Lake of the Cherokee in northeastern Oklahoma.

"Marshall," he told me one day as we sat looking out toward the lake and the blue autumn skies above it, "I never realized how important golf was to Blake. During the years he was sick, golf was the thing he looked forward to the most."

I knew Blake well, and one of the things that always struck me about him was his devotion to the rules of the game. Even in the coldest winter months, he never improved his lie or took a gimme that wasn't sitting right on the lip. Something about the finality of the rules eased his mind, took away the pressure from all the gray areas of life. A few weeks after Blake's death I woke up from a dream. In my dream Blake and Mickey Mantle, another dear friend who found peace through golf, were playing a match in heaven. Talk about target golf. They were teeing up on one cloud and hitting tremendous shots across broad reaches of sky to other clouds.

"Now don't let me see you rolling the ball over," Blake told Mickey. "Up here we always play by the rules."

When I told this to Steve, he smiled. "That's Blake, all right," he said to me. "I'm glad to know he's doing well up there."

And I believe he really is. The character he revealed on the golf course continues to live on. It's something we'll always be able to remember, and Steve will have a piece of his son with him during every round he plays for the rest of his life.

Walk Through the Front Door

Golf is an invitation to join the greatest club of all. When you play golf - particularly when you play with pride and etiquette and work to sharpen your skills - you will find yourself meeting all types of people. More than that, you'll get to know these people. That's why golf is so important to business. It's not so much that big deals get made on the course - those deals generally take time and effort that you'd rather not steal from your golf game. But golf gives business people the chance to build even better relationships with their clients and colleagues. You don't have to be a great player to reap these benefits. You just have to respect and love the game. My brother has played golf for many years. He's not the best ball-striker in the world, but his putting has made him a valuable member of many scramble teams, and that's been a big plus for his business.

Golf won't necessarily make you a success in business or in life, but it can give you a great head start. On the golf course, the CEO and the mail room clerk are on equal footing. They shed their roles and play a game they love. When they come together at the 19th hole, they've gained a little understanding about each other as people, not as titles. That's what I mean when I say that golf lets you go in the front door. Your love for the game will leave an impression on everyone you ever meet on the golf course, and making a good impression never hurt anyone.

People who love golf like to spend time with other people who love golf. It's just that simple. Today, golf even brings nations closer together. I saw in the newspaper that the President played golf with the president of Argentina during a recent trip to South America. Don't you think their conversation came just a little easier on a golf course than it might have at a big round table surrounded by microphones and political aides?

The community of golf has a heart of gold. Is there any other sport that devotes so much time and energy to raising money for charities? From local tournaments to the PGA Tour, golfers come together and use their enthusiasm for the game to make contributions to their cities and to the less fortunate. Golf is a privilege and a gift that we've been lucky enough to share. It's up to us to make sure that the gift does some good for others.

Crossing the Generation Gap

Very little in this world stays the same. In the 65 years that I've been playing golf, I've seen wars come and go, fortunes won and lost, cities rise and fall. Sometimes I think it would be impossible to digest the change going on around me all the time if I couldn't fall back to golf. The game may not have kept me from growing older, but it's sure as hell kept me from feeling old.

Golf has kept me young because it's kept me in touch with kids. No other sport brings the generations together the way golf does. When I was a boy, Oklahoma was still a rough and ready frontier. I learned its history on the golf course, playing with old-timers who had seen the birth of the state. We were friends, those older folks and me. Every morning I would sling my clubs over my shoulder and board a Greyhound bus in Quapaw, paying a dime for the short ride to Baxter Springs, Kansas. I'd stay until it was dark. The lessons I learned on those long summer days have stayed with me forever. They have turned into lessons for thousands of kids I've had the great fortune of knowing and teaching all these years.

People ask me all the time when they should start their kids at golf, and I tell them, "as soon as they show an interest in it."

The family that plays together stays together. That's been my experience. In a world that moves as quickly as ours does today, there are very few activities that allow you to spend four hours of true quality time with the people you love. Golf fills those four hours with so many opportunities for sharing, learning and growing. Children who play golf with their parents will look forward to spending time with their parents for the rest of their lives. Even as you grow through the trying times of adolesence and young adulthood, the golf course will give you the chance to retreat from the pressures of living and just enjoy being together. And isn't that what a family is all about?

Because of the young people I've known through golf, I've never worried about the future. I know we're going to be just fine. In a lot of ways, they've taught me as much as I've taught them, and I think these kids yearn for the tradition and history that golf provides. I consider golf a gift, one that you can give to your children and their children. Not only is golf a great activity that they'll enjoy all their lives, but it has a code of values and ethics they can live by. I still start all my junior lessons by letting the kids know that they'll use "sir" and "ma'am" when talking with the adults they meet through golf. Golf provides a living classroom for teaching discipline and hard work, achievement and the graceful handling of loss. Remember that kids are born into this world with no direction. They depend on you to give it to them. Introducing a kid to golf is your chance to open up a world of possibilities.

Golf teaches kids to be "people smart." It breaks down the walls between the generations. Every golf course has a few colorful characters who just want to be a part of the young people who are learning the game. They watch over them, helping them learn golf skills, reproaching them for violations of the rules or for losing their temper. They tell them the stories that all golfers should know - the legends of great players and bygone times. Go home and watch the news on your television tonight. Kids today have to deal with too much of the negative. Golf - and the people they meet through the game - offer something more positive.

Beyond all of that, golf requires dedication and energy, something kids just naturally possess. When a youngster is serious about improving his or her golf game, there's not a lot of time for trouble. You play all day and you look forward to playing well the next day. That's a mighty strong incentive for staying off the streets. The confidence kids get from being a part of something as difficult and rewarding as golf will carry over into everything they do. I've never been afraid of anyone or any situation where I had to mix with people I didn't know. I credit golf for that.

Finally, golf is forever. You already know that - that's why you're reading this book. When you give a child the gift of golf, you're giving something that will last a lifetime. I always encouraged my kids to play other sports like football, baseball and basketball. Those sports teach many lessons as well, but you can't play them forever. Golf, on the other hand, will always be there.

I'm 71 years old, and there's not a day that goes by that I don't find out something new about myself thanks to golf. When I met Tom Ferrell, I had no intention of ever doing a book on golf. I preferred the one-on-one of personal instruction. But as we began working, I realized that I had something to say. I hope you've found something in these pages to take with you as you continue your journey through the greatest game of all.

I know I have.

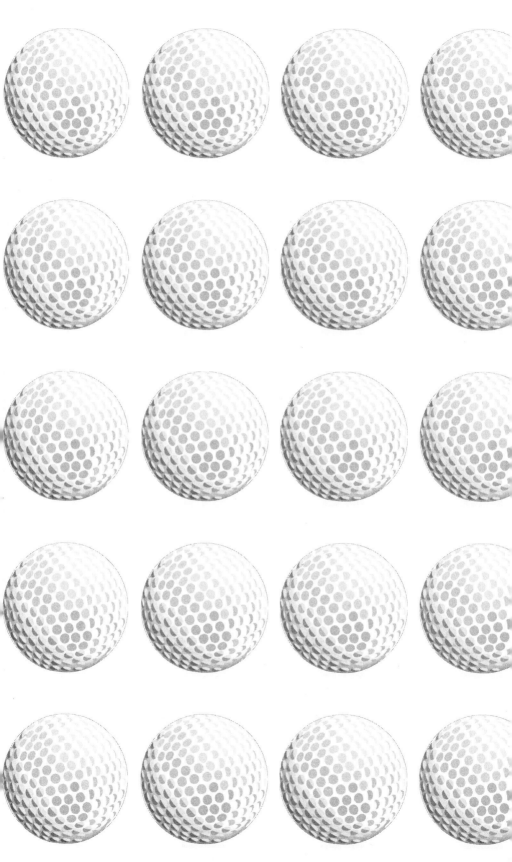